ONE HUNDRED AND FIVE YEARS YOUNG

Copyright © 2023 by Cora Hoberman. All rights reserved. Printed in the United States of America. No part of this book may be used or reproduced in any manner whatsoever without written permission except in the case of brief quotations included in critical articles and reviews. For information, address Permissions@ CitrinePublishing.com.

Limit of Liability/Disclaimer of Warranty: The author has tried to recreate events, locales and conversations from family memories of them. In order to maintain anonymity in some instances, she may have changed some identifying characteristics and details such as names, physical properties, occupations and places of residence. While the publisher and author have used their best efforts in preparing this book, they make no representations or warranties with respect to the accuracy or completeness of the contents of this book and specifically disclaim any implied warranties of merchantability or fitness for a particular purpose. In the event you use any of the information in the book for yourself, which is your constitutional right, the author and publisher assume no responsibility for your actions. The views expressed in this work are solely those of the author and do not necessarily reflect the views of the publisher.

Editing by Jaime Cox • Cover by Rolf Busch • Back Cover Painting by Meron Philo • Family photos used with permission • Photo of S.S. United States by Michael Muchmore via WikiCommons: https://commons.wikimedia.org/wiki/File:S.S._United_States.jpg

Library of Congress Cataloging-in-Publication Data
One Hundred and Five Years Young: A Daughter's Memoir
Cora Hoberman
p. cm.
Paperback ISBN: 978-1-947708-60-0
Ebook ISBN: 978-1-947708-65-5
Library of Congress Control Number: 2023908698
First Edition, July 2023

State College, Pennsylvania, USA
(828) 585 - 7030
www.CitrinePublishing.com

ONE HUNDRED AND FIVE YEARS YOUNG

A Daughter's Memoir

CORA HOBERMAN

Also by Cora Hoberman

Snowbirds

For Penny

One Mother's Day, I gave Mom a flowery card that read, "For My Sweet Mother."

"Oh no," she said, after reading it. "That's not for me. I'm not sweet. I'm strong."

Introduction

IT HAS BEEN A CHALLENGE to write this story—a struggle to encapsulate my mom's many years of living and to do justice to her very active one hundred and five years. Instead of attempting to present her life in chronological order, I decided to focus on the meaningful periods. My purpose in telling her story is to shine a light on her ability to age so successfully and with such positivity.

Prologue

"DO YOU REMEMBER MY MOTHER?" I asked Ichiro as he walked through the Manhattan Plaza lobby. My eyes landed on him, a Japanese neighbor who was once a Kabuki dancer.

"Of course I do. She was such a legend. She was so active and alert, even at one hundred years old."

"Mom used to tell me that you brought her gifts of fruit from Chinatown from time to time," I said. He nodded. "Sometimes it was a bunch of huge red cherries, she told me, and sometimes the sweetest melons she had ever tasted." He nodded again with a smile. "She enjoyed that so much," I said, looking at him again.

"I'm so glad." With that, Ichiro bowed a goodbye and went on his way. He had a quiet, calm reticence and I found myself pausing as I watched him walk away, grateful for his kindness to Mom in her older years.

As an eighty-year-old in 1984, Mom had moved into apartment 7P in Manhattan Plaza. Built in 1977, Manhattan Plaza was located in Hell's Kitchen, two blocks from Times Square. The enormous complex consists of two, forty-five story buildings at opposite ends of West 43rd Street, housing a total of two thousand residents. Most tenants who live there work in the performing arts. Getting an apartment was, and still remains, extremely desirable, not just because of its proximity to Broadway, but primarily due to its affordability. In order to be eligible, one needs to be employed in the "business" as an actor, writer, musician, stagehand, etc. Mom's job as an usher at a Broadway theater had made her a candidate, and her membership in the International Alliance of Theatrical Stage Employees union (IATSE) clinched the deal. There's a notion out there that ushers are volunteers, working to see the shows for free, but in most cases, Broadway theater ushers are salaried workers who can receive medical and other benefits, as long as they belong to the union.

Although the building is affordable, it is also equitable. Those with lower incomes pay lower rents. As one's income increases, so does their rent. And so, Manhattan Plaza is home to many who are starting out in their careers—some of whom will progress into stardom and move to Hollywood. In contrast, many Broadway actors remain in the building, paying top rent.

So that's a glimpse as to why these apartments are so desirable and the wait list is so long. Mom waited for nine years. The idea that she might get an apartment "anytime soon" had long left her consciousness. So when she got the call from Susan Bernstein from the rental office, saying, "We have an apartment for you!" Mom called me right away to tell me, and I was so happy and excited for her. But she was a bit hesitant at first.

"I'm not sure if I can do it," she told me. "Just the thought of packing everything up is overwhelming."

A few weeks prior, while crossing the street, a panel truck had bumped into her as it was turning the corner and knocked her down.

Margaret, her work partner, called me after the incident.

"Cora, you have to come into New York. Your mother had an accident." At the time, I was living way out in Suffolk county. My husband drove me to the rail station and fortunately, a train quickly arrived, taking me on the one-and-a-half hour ride on the Long Island Railroad into Penn Station. I arrived at midnight.

I worried about her during the entire ride, not knowing what to expect when I got there.

When I finally arrived at her apartment, she opened the door in her white cotton night gown, looking tired, frail, and old. I'd never seen her like that. Mom was always the energetic Energizer Bunny, and always dressed to the nines. But that day, I saw her true age.

We sat to talk. "The truck didn't injure me, it just knocked me down," she explained. "They took some X-rays at the hospital and luckily, nothing is broken. It was such just a shock. All I did was step off the curb when the light changed and he came barreling through. I'm so upset that I don't think I can move to a new building now."

"Of course! If you don't want to. Let's sit down and relax and wait for Marvin to bring your prescription. I'll make you a cup of coffee while we wait," I said. Mom could drink coffee any time of the day or night, even before bedtime. It calmed her down and didn't affect her sleep.

We talked about the pros and cons of taking the apartment. She had been complaining recently about her present space that was quite small and didn't have a real kitchen (the stove and sink being in the entry hall). Being the trooper she was, she eventually decided to make the move.

Once settled in, she loved everything about her new apartment. She loved her view straight down 9th Avenue. The New York City skyline was mesmerizing at night. I could sit and gaze at it for hours whenever I visited her. Neighbors welcomed her onto their floor—a Manhattan Plaza tradition, designed to make new residents feel comfortable in their new surroundings—by signing a card, wishing her well in her new home. Especially endearing were Matthew, a young playwright, his wife Tillie, and their son and daughter in the corner apartment on Mom's floor. They became wonderful friends to Mom and helped her in so many ways.

Long, dark-haired Marina was an actress who repaired jewelry on the side. Scott, Mom's next-door neighbor, was a voice coach who often had clients waiting in the hallway, sitting cross-legged on the grey carpet until he was ready to see them.

It was an exceptional building—more than just a place to live. It was a community that fostered many notable people. You never knew who you might bump into in the elevator or down in the lobby. Al Pacino, James Earl Jones, Terrence Howard, and Nell Carter had all lived there over various years. I heard about Mom's sightings when we spoke on the phone. "You'll never believe who I saw in the elevator today! Angela Lansbury!" she'd tell me, excitement in her voice.

We both saw Andrea McArdle when she played "Annie" at the Alvin Theater. She and her family lived in the west building on 10th Avenue. Alicia Keys grew up in that building as well. The actual person the character "Kramer," was based upon, lived across the hall from Larry David, cocreator of *Seinfeld*, in the 10th Avenue building, too.

Of course, not everyone was a star. Many others didn't make it big, but some were fortunate to get small parts in TV series or movies. It was fun for Mom to be watching a TV show and unexpectedly spot one of her neighbors playing a role. It was fun for me as well, as one night while I was watching *Sex and the City*, I spotted her friend Delores in a scene, sitting in a therapist's waiting room, while Carrie Bradshaw sat two chairs away.

The building provided a supportive opportunity for those in the field. Everyone knew Samuel L. Jackson when he worked as a Manhattan Plaza security guard. He was just a struggling actor back then.

At eighty, Mom was still working. She enjoyed her job as an usherette in the Uris Theater doing six shows a week and she didn't have the time to socialize. Then when she retired from the theater at ninety, she had more time to meet others.

I recently saw one of Mom's old neighbors, Marina. She told me about the special friendship she and Mom had enjoyed.

"Fran often called me in the evening, asking me to help her take off her necklace, because she couldn't undo the latch. 'Of course, I'll be right over.' I would say," Marina said. "We were neighbors on the seventh floor. I lived in 7N, two doors down from her. Fran was in her nineties and I was in my forties. Even though we were in different stages of life, we connected. And we developed a good friendship. She would also call to say, 'I'm having a cup of tea, would you like to join me?' Then we would talk for hours while sipping Earl Grey from the flowered bone China cups, which she had purchased in various antique stores. 'Wow, it's 3:00 am—I'd better go home,' I remember saying more than once, while chatting in her living room.

"Fran enjoyed wearing her jewelry; each item was a collectible piece she had purchased carefully. She found them at flea markets in New York and also in Paris. Actually, that's how we met, because she needed some necklaces to be repaired and I was able to do that for her. She loved her jewelry, but her hats were her most important possessions.

"One night when I visited, she took down all the hat boxes and modeled each hat for me. She presented them as treasures that she had acquired over the years. They were like an expression of her personality and past life. We didn't just talk about hats. We got deep into life and talked about more personal things. Often she reminisced by telling me about the vital life decisions she had made, including when she divorced your dad. 'Make the best decisions you can,' she told me, 'and then deal with the consequences when you need to.'

"That was her philosophy: 'Move ahead and don't get stuck in the past.'

"I felt comfortable enough to bare my feelings with her. My life had not been easy. As a child I had polio and still have difficulty walking. Most of the time, I used my wheelchair to get around, but Fran would encourage me to walk. 'Don't sit on your chair all the time. Walk! I know you can walk,' she'd tell me.

"We talked about men and we talked about sex. 'How long do women desire sex?' I asked her once. 'As long as they're capable,' she shared. I confessed one night that I'd like to have a man in my life. I'm a single mother with a young daughter and am separated from her father. My physical disability stood in the way of actively trying to meet someone. 'You're a beautiful girl. Maybe you haven't been ready for a relationship 'til now. Open your heart and your mind to receive love.' Those were strong words and I wasn't convinced it could happen so easily. But Fran was a wise woman, so I just decided to be more open with people. And then I did meet someone. Someone nice!"

"The old actors," as they were called, would sit at the tables outside the cafes that lined the street. They would sit for hours, telling stories and relating old memories. Often, they'd buy a cup of coffee or a sandwich, allowing them to sit for a while. Mom also found a seat at one of those tables. Mostly she listened to their stories but did not share much about herself or her previous life. She made a few friends in the building and sometimes they'd sit together outside of Good and Plenty To Go, which had what I would call "gourmet" take-out.

Most days Mom sat, nursed a cup of coffee, and munched on a Danish. At times, for special people, the counter servers would bring the food outside to those waiting. Alonso was one of these servers, who took a liking to Mom. He was a slender, dark-haired, gay young man from Columbia who was very fashion conscious and admired Mom's clothes. "I love your hat. Where did you get that pin?" he'd inquire. He appeared to be fascinated by her. Sometimes he would sit down at the table with her—although the store manager wasn't happy about it. But Alonso marched to his own drummer and had his own way of looking at life. Very quickly they became fast friends.

He invited her to parties with his pals. He came over to cook for her. I think he borrowed money from her on occasion but he usually paid it back (hopefully). She had a swell time with him. All his friends admired her and seemed to enjoy spending time with this elegant, elderly lady Alonso had introduced them to. When they played music and danced, she danced in her seat, to their delight. I guess it was like spending time with a really hip grandma. Alonso lived nearby on West 45th Street but wasn't happy with his apartment. Mom once described it as a "small dark hole in the wall." And so, sometimes he would invite his friends to her place. One day Alonso told her that he was planning to join a gay parade to be held at Washington Square Park. "I'm going to wear a pink chiffon dress," he said. "Can I borrow your pink hat with the large brim to go with it?"

"Yes! Try it on to see how it fits," she said with delight.

At ninety-three she suffered a fall, causing her to use a cane. Of course, she chose an attractive one. In her late nineties, she began to use a walker. She bought one with big wheels. It was one of the early Rollators, manufactured in Sweden. She maneuvered it as if she were a professional race car driver.

Mom with her brother Jack in New York.

Chapter 1

Becoming Fran

THERE WAS A TINY FIVE-YEAR-OLD wearing an earring in one ear. Her name was Funya, in Russian, though Fega, her Yiddish name, was what her parents chose to call her. Once she was in the US, everyone called her Fannie. Then later on, she adopted the more Americanized versions, Frances or Fran, which she thought more suitable for the professional woman she became.

Mom was born in 1904 in Zhytomyr, a city near Kiev, at the time a part of Russia. But the family later moved to Odessa. After the breakup of the Soviet Union in 1991, Odessa became part of the independent state of Ukraine.

She and my grandparents, Ida and Pasa, lived in a small cottage together with her four brothers—Willie, Nathan, Sam, Jack—and Lily, her younger sister. The earliest picture I have of her was taken at the photo department in the city of Odessa, showing a tiny, five-year-old, brown-eyed, brown-haired little girl, wearing an earring in only one ear. In the photo, she and her sister sit upon an ornate wooden chair.

Most Russian Jews at the time lived in small market towns called *shtetls*. (Something like we

Mom on the right at five years old with her sister, Lily. Photo taken In Odessa, Russia.

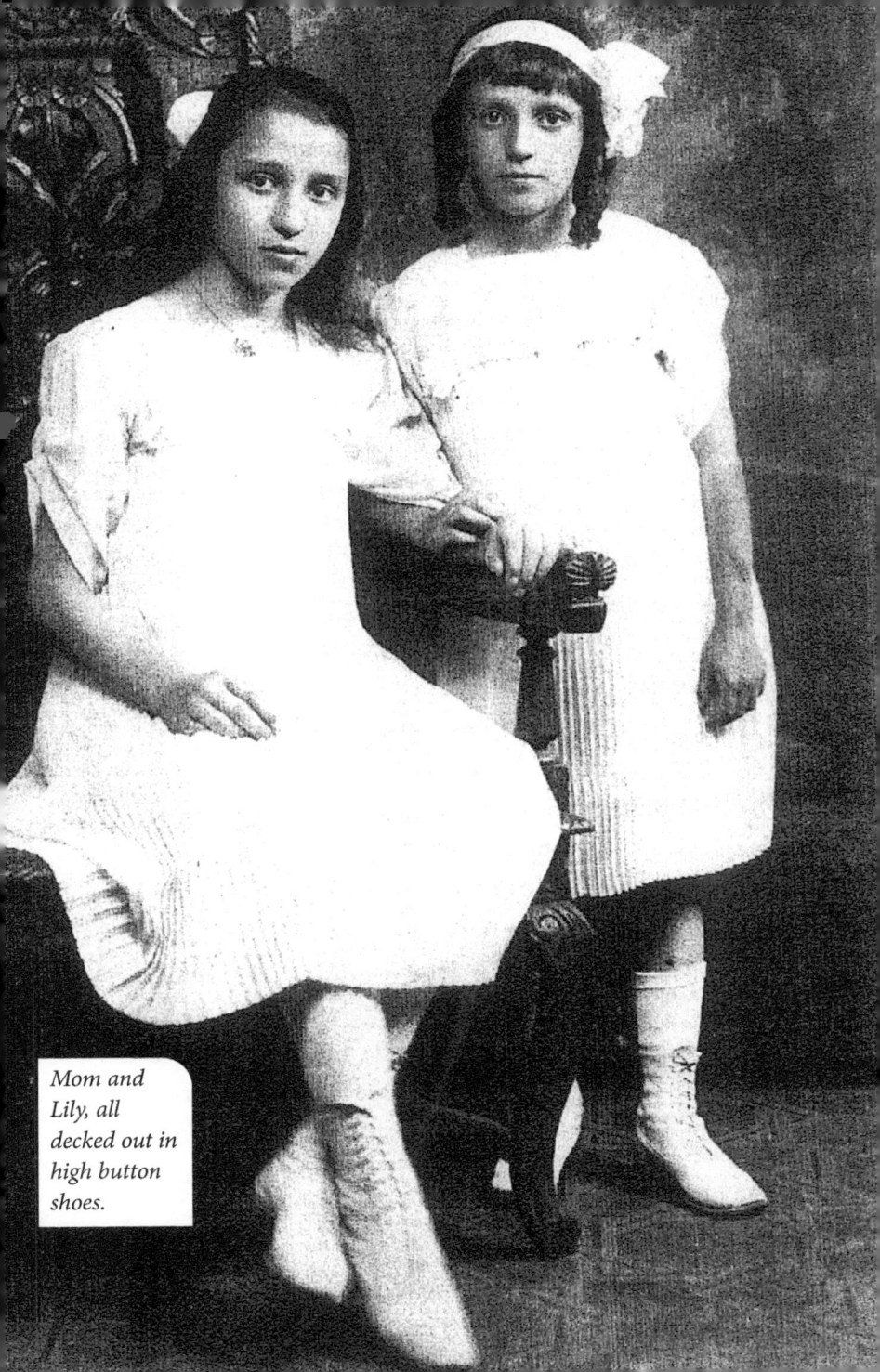

Mom and Lily, all decked out in high button shoes.

saw, in a very romanticized version, in *Fiddler on the Roof*.)

I can only assume that my family did also.

The *shtetl* had unpaved streets, which turned to mud in the rain. Homes were made of wood and the use of outhouses created unsanitary conditions.

Many of the residents who lived there were poor. What saved them from starvation and being evicted from their homes was Jewish charity. *Tzadekah* ("charity" in Yiddish) is considered a moral obligation by observant Jewish people to provide financial help to those in need. Even the poor at times would help others who were struggling.

Although they all spoke Russian, Yiddish was the primary language of the *shtetls*.

Tsar Nicholas II was in command at the time (1874 to 1917). He was the last emperor of Russia and during the period of his reign, the Jewish people had a very difficult time.

Odessa was part of an area known as The Pale of Settlement. Over 90 percent of Russian Jews had to live within what was known as "The Pale"—a vast ghetto of approximately 400,000 square miles, extending from the Baltic Sea to the Black Sea.

Not only was their geography determined by the government, they also had to live under strict curfews and were only permitted to engage in certain trades. Studying to become a professional such as a lawyer or teacher was forbidden. According to historian Albert S. Lindemann, "Many impoverished Jewish craftsman, artisans, apprentices, and petty merchants lived in the Pale."

The Jews were also prohibited from owning their own homes.

In addition, they had to contend with the large-scale, anti-Jewish riots otherwise known as *pogroms*, during which many were robbed and beaten.

In 1905, the worst of them all happened in Odessa, when thousands of Jews were killed.

Mom often spoke to me about the Cossacks, the soldiers who were employed by the Tsar and charged with control of the Jews. She remembered them as threatening figures on horseback, wearing big fur hats.

"They had long black boots and carried guns. My brothers were always frightened to leave our house at night because if they went into the streets after curfew or wandered outside of the area, the Cossacks would lash at them with their whips," she recalled. It was a memory instilled into each of her brothers—a memory they shared with their own children.

By 1913, the family had had enough of Mother Russia. The government had placed stringent restrictions on their every move, making it more and more difficult for Pasa, my grandfather, to earn a living and put food on the table. Due to the harsh, nightmarish life they had been forced to live, over two million Russian Jews had to leave their homes.

So, like so many of their neighbors, my grandparents decided to emigrate to the United States. On the Ellis Island website, I was able to locate their ship's passenger lists. My grandfather, a quiet, soft-spoken man, took a brave step and was the first member of my family to depart. It was on the *S.S. Noordam*, a Holland-American ship. Months later, Mom's eldest brother, Willie (Velvel), followed. They planned to get settled in the new country, look for work, and find a residence fit for the entire family.

The Gerstein's, friends from their neighborhood in Odessa, had already made the pilgrimage and had agreed to act as sponsors for my family members, thereby allowing them to enter the US.

My grandmother, my mother, my uncles (three of her brothers), and my aunt (her younger sister), were the last to leave. Thinking about what they did, I'm awed by the courage it must have taken for my grandmother to pack up four children and leave their home for such a long journey to a foreign place. I only wish I had asked her about it years ago when I had the opportunity.

First, they had to make their way by rail to Rotterdam, which took several days, before they could reach the port from which their boat would depart. For many nights, those waiting to get on the ship stayed in huge, crowded, and dirty Quonset-like huts along with so many other families until finally they got permission to board their ship.

According to records, most families had to sell all their possessions to pay for their transport. Representatives from the shipping lines were sent out to the small towns to offer package deals to those interested in emigrating. The deals included the railroad ticket, lodging, and the ship passage, for one all-inclusive price.

On the day they departed, records of the *S.S. Noordam* list 286 first-class passengers, 292 second-class passengers, and 1800 third-class passengers, my family being a part of the latter. Being so closely packed together with others in third class (otherwise known as "steerage") must have been a nightmare.

"I remember the dark. We were all pushed together and the rocking of the boat made me sick," Mom told me once. Although nine years old, she didn't remember much else about the voyage.

Finally, after crossing the North Atlantic Ocean in the horrendous belly of the ship, they arrived on Ellis Island. Those who had staterooms in first or second class were permitted to freely leave the ship—those in steerage were moved to the Great Hall where their physical and mental abilities were observed and judged as they underwent a thorough inspection process. Obviously, my family made it through. Reportedly, only two percent of all immigrants were denied entrance into the United States and deported.

I can't imagine the culture shock they must have experienced when they arrived. Amongst thousands of people looking for their relatives, they had to find Willie (Velvel), who had come to America earlier with Pasa, as he waited on the dock, searching for their faces. Finally, there he was to greet them.

What a sight for sore eyes he most likely was. It must have been such a relief for them to be with a family member after the crowding together with strangers on the ship and while they went through the processing on Ellis Island. I can picture tears rolling down my grandmother Ida's face as they took turns hugging and kissing Willie while bombarding him with questions.

"Can we go to our home now?" they all wanted to know.

"Yes, of course. Let's go," Willie told them. "We are going to take the streetcar." That brought them to the Lower East Side. It was an area teeming with Jewish immigrants. By 1910, according to the Library of Congress, millions of Jews, mostly poor, had emigrated to this area. At the time it was considered the "most crowded neighborhood on the planet."

With eyes wide open they stared out the trolley windows, observing the automobiles intermixed with the horse-drawn carriages. When they arrived at their stop, the girls held hands as they stepped down from the trolley car. The boys helped their mother off.

"Here it is, Mama," Willie said when they stood in front of number 324 on East 9th Street.

Craning their necks, they all looked up to see the red-brick building with a black cornice at its top. (Note: Years later Mom frequently enjoyed making visits to this building where she had grown up. At the time, that section of 9th Street was part of the East Village. She could stop for a chocolate babka at the 9th Street Bakery—which had occupied the same space for eighty-seven years—or she could have had a bowl of borscht at one of the Ukrainian restaurants lining 2nd Avenue.)

As they walked single file up the white marble steps to reach the 4th floor, each of them held firmly onto the curved metal banister. They had never been in an apartment building before, nor had they climbed so many stairs.

A mix of awe and excitement overcame them when Willie turned the key to unlock the door of their two-room apartment. In the kitchen they lifted the top off the icebox. "No more putting the milk outside the window," Lily laughed.

They peered curiously into the stove which was fueled by coal instead of the kindling wood they had used back in Odessa.

Eight members of the family were to live in this compact unit. Out the window they saw an alley with clotheslines strung across to the adjacent tenement. The toilet down the hall was shared with all the other residents of the building.

The apartment was so small that Mom's youngest brother, Jack, had to sleep in the bathtub that was located in the kitchen. "I hated sleeping in that cold box," he confided to his daughter, my cousin Maxene, when he described their living conditions. It was Grandma Ida who had determined the sleeping arrangements. A petite woman, she actually dominated the family and made all the household decisions. Although uneducated, she was a very bright woman. In the following days and weeks, the family had to learn to live an entirely different way of life.

The densely packed district of tenements was easily a frightening, noisy, and cramped place, but still, it was safer than the Russia they had left. At

Grandma Ida, Mom's mother.

least they had escaped the political situation and the dangers of the pogroms. Reportedly, on the street, pushcarts were everywhere. Peddlers yelled to advertise their wares. Women pushed and shoved to make their way through. Noisy children played in the gutters. Thousands of pushcarts clogged those streets of the Lower East Side. As chaotic as it seemed, they had to accept it as their new home. My grandmother had to learn to navigate through the crowds, to learn which carts had the best prices. All their food came from these vendors who sold fresh vegetables, even knishes and pickles. It was the most economical way to shop.

When fall came, it was time for school. Fannie took hold of her little sister's hand as they crossed Second Avenue to reach their local elementary school. She was nine years old and Lily was seven. I don't know what grade they went to, but Mom admitted, "It was hard for me to learn and keep up with the class. Sometimes the teacher even threw erasers at my head if I didn't know the answers. But Lily learned more quickly than I did. She was younger and picked up the language more easily than me. I only made it to eighth grade." Mom told me this with a note of regret in her voice. She had a thirst for knowledge all her life and I believe she was sorry to have missed the opportunity to learn in her

Mom's brothers, Willie, Sam and Nathen.

early years. However, in my research I became aware that many young girls during that period did not complete an education, mostly because they needed to go to work. Attending school had become an embarrassment and a humiliation with her teacher berating her. So going to work seemed a positive as well a necessary thing to do.

Pasa became a peddler who sold shoes. "They weren't new shoes," Mom told me. He bought hardly used shoes from people and sold them to others. I thought it was interesting that he had no store or even a pushcart in which to display his wares. He set up on a street between two buildings, displaying his shoes right on the sidewalk. Hard as he tried, Fran's father couldn't earn enough peddling shoes, so other family members needed to contribute to their income.

Her brother, my uncle Sam (who eventually became a handbag manufacturer and was known as the family millionaire) remembered going to work at a very young age. He told his daughter, my cousin Nikki, "Grandma gave me only one banana to feed me for the rest of the day. And I had to go out and earn a living for the family. Can you believe it?"

Soon it became Fannie's turn to bring in some money.

There was a burgeoning interest in fashion beginning to emerge in the city, and Fran started to take notice of what others were wearing. Hats attracted her the most and so she sought a job in the millinery business. She started small—learning how to block hats on forms. Later she progressed to design by adding ribbons and feathers to already-shaped hats. Over the years, she worked for many small companies but was most proud of the time she spent at Lilly Daché, a well-known French milliner and designer of the day.

From that time forward, hats became her passion and a signature of her style. Anybody who saw her walking down her Manhattan Street, even many years later, could always tell it was Mom. She wore a different hat every day, each more beautiful than the last: furs in the winter, patterned or striped in the fall, straws encircled by ribbons for summer. She knew just how to tilt them on her head and which best matched her outfit of the day. She knew how to alter and redesign them by adding a flower or a pin. She knew how to steam them when the brim had gotten out of shape.

"Nice hat," she would frequently hear from friends or strangers as she went about her day.

Chapter 2
Settlement Houses

IN 1922, FRAN WAS EIGHTEEN years old, and it was just two years after women had gained the right to vote in the United States.

Up on the roof of the tenement, free from her cramped apartment, she could spend time talking to her friends. It was where they were able to meet and chat. Sometimes they posed for the camera by forming a tower of three, with each girl sitting upon the other's shoulders. They would come after work, still wearing their finest outfits. As usual, Fran dressed in high style, often wearing a suit and a large-brimmed hat and sporting a fur scarf with the actual animal head still attached—hard to believe, but it was a fashion in its day. (Good thing PETA wasn't around yet.)

On a sweltering hot summer day, they would take the subway to Coney Island and spend the day at the Washington Baths, one of the many bathhouses proliferating Coney Island and Brighton Beach. This was where the average New Yorker could spend an afternoon taking a dip in the Atlantic Ocean or just enjoy the rays. All Fran and her friends needed to do was to purchase a locker where they could change

Mom with her friends on the roof.

into their swimsuits—they could even rent a bathing suit for the day.

When the Stillwell Avenue Subway Station opened in 1919, Coney Island became the "watering place for all the people." A ticket cost only 5¢ and thus Coney Island became known as "The Nickel Empire." For another nickel they might get a hotdog at Nathan's.

Rockaway Beach was also a favorite spot. A picture in one of Mom's photo albums shows her wearing a long, black, wool bathing suit, in a jumper style. It's what they wore back in the day, so as to not reveal too much of the body. Bikinis weren't in yet. She and her friends were very active. They went boating in Van Cortlandt Park in the Bronx or hiking on Bear Mountain.

They also spent time at a Lower East Side Settlement House.

"It wasn't the well-known Henry Street Settlement House," she once told me. But it might possibly have been the University Settlement, which was also on the Lower East Side, originally located on Eldridge Street.

George and Ira Gershwin, Jacob Javits, and Abraham Beame were among the many alumni of University House, according to University Settlement records. Settlement houses were created in what was

Mom on the beach.

called the "Progressive Era," when reformers' goals were to create educational reform and to lobby for improved social policies.

The housing was built for the new immigrants, who came pouring in by the thousands, from Eastern Europe and from Italy. Most of them, like my grandfather and my uncles, worked in the clothing industry. They lived in the wall-to-wall, five- and-six story, red-brick tenement buildings which covered large stretches of lower Manhattan. Mostly they were poor families suffering poverty and hardship due to their low-paid jobs and crowded living conditions.

At the settlement houses, young middle-class college graduates volunteered to serve as what were characterized as reformers, to help those in need. Their service has been compared to that of the Peace Corps. The settlement workers offered day care and created the first kindergarten program in New York City. They taught the new immigrants to speak English.

Once a month, the settlement house held a dance, and this is what most attracted Mom—the settlement house is where she met my father. She enjoyed the foxtrot, a popular dance at the time. There were two variations of the foxtrot: a slow version done at about forty measures per minute and a fast version, done at more than fifty measures per minute. But most of all, she loved the Peabody.

Originally called the "fast foxtrot," the Peabody was named after New York policeman Lieutenant William Frank Peabody. He was a large man who especially liked dancing the fast foxtrot. Because of his girth, he was unable to hold his partner directly in front of him, so he would hold her on his right side. As this dance was based on an unusual dance position for the female partners, it led to some unique steps. It was brisk and covered lots of floor space, responding to tunes such as "Ain't She Sweet," "When the Saints Go Marching In," and "Yes, We Have No Bananas."

She loved to dance and remembered having some wonderful dance partners. They traveled around the floor with ease, leading her in long gliding strides, sometimes adding promenades and simple turns as the dance progressed. She took to it because it was challenging and fast with interesting variations. She danced it well because she was graceful and quick. When I was in my teens, she once showed me some of the steps, but I never danced it as well as Mom did.

In 1923, on the Lower East Side of New York, Mom met her friends, Mildred and Esther, on the stoop downstairs. The settlement house was hosting a dance that night and each girl wore her best dress. They were always excited about going, chattering as they walked over, and busy wondering who would be there and which boys would ask for a dance. People gathered not only to dance, but to socialize, often with the hope of meeting a future spouse.

Mom and her father, taken on the roof of their apartment building on the Lower East Side.

Mom in a large-brimmed hat.

Dad's father Charles, wearing his New York City police uniform.

Mom and Dad in love.

Chapter 3
Dad

OVER THE YEARS, MOM HAD many opportunities to reminisce. She told me once, "I had lots of great partners who enjoyed dancing with me, but they were mostly young men from the neighborhood. But one night, a man named David approached and asked me to dance. He wasn't as good a dancer as the others, but he was very good looking—different from the others." The men she knew were Russian Jews: short, with dark hair and dark eyes. Dave stood tall. He had light brown hair, green eyes, and a shy smile. It turned out he was also Jewish—just not the typical Jewish man she had grown up with and had seen all her life. She found him intriguing and thought about him a lot. At the next dance she went to, her pulse quickened when she spotted him across the room. He was quiet but she hoped that he was interested in her.

"This wasn't his neighborhood, but he came back anyway." She told me she had made a decision to actively pursue him. "I really liked him—so much that I ran after him," she confided. It wasn't just his looks that appealed; he also represented a way out of the ghetto and into assimilation.

"Would you like to take a walk with me this Sunday? We can go to Central Park," he finally asked.

"Yes, that would be nice," Mom replied. She recalled putting her arm through his as they strolled about, watching the horse-drawn carriages, and passing by the Bethesda Fountain. Sunday quickly became their day to be with one another. She introduced him to her friends and he joined in their adventures in the city. He liked to sing and belonged to a barbershop quartet, singing four-part harmony. Mom was invited to all their performances, which she loved. Even though they never had a formal engagement, the idea that they would marry was understood by both of them.

After a year together, they told their parents of their intentions. Their families were so different. Both were Jewish, but living very different lives; Mom's followed all the religious holidays and traditions and they kept a kosher home, while Dad's (David's) family was barely observant. According to Mom, her eyebrows raised in astonishment, "Dave did have a bar mitzvah, but with a minstrel performance. No one ever heard of doing that."

The two sets of parents finally met. It's hard for me to picture my maternal Grandmother Ida with her long, white, braided hair atop her long black dress, meeting my paternal Grandmother Rose, dressed in the latest style of the day.

"We got married in 1926 in a small restaurant on 2nd Avenue." Mom told me they could only afford to invite family and some very close friends. Dad was born in the United States—his parents had emigrated from Berlin like many other German Jews who came to the states in the late 1800s. While Mom's family still lived in a tenement on the Lower East Side, his had their own private home in the Bronx.

His father, Charles, a police officer, rode a bicycle throughout the NYC streets while on patrol. He became a member of the Shomrin Society, created to protect and support the Jewish policemen who worked in New York City. It was formed after several discriminatory incidents had occurred against the first Jewish cops in New York, and the men felt a need to join together for support.

Mom described her mother-in-law Rose as "great in the kitchen" and remembered her as not only being an excellent cook, but also a great housekeeper. Although Rose appeared to be just a house frau, she had been brought up in a professional home. Her family had money. She had enough to help with the purchases and to share with her grandchildren later in life.

Mother was like a sponge in those years; she wanted to learn and to assimilate to the US. She observed and imitated Rose's recipes. They weren't the Russian, kosher, Jewish foods she had grown up eating, like borscht or latkes. Instead, they represented a more American style of cooking: eye-of-round round roast beef cooked till rosy pink, baked noodles layered with Velveeta cheese along with lots of fresh vegetables. These were the foods we later enjoyed at our dinner table.

After they married, they moved in with my father's parents, Rose and Charles, to their Bronx home. Mom was anxious to be involved and to help out with her new family. They took advantage of that and used her almost "as a maid" she told me. As an immigrant she was beneath them, they thought. At times they even resorted to calling her a kike. (According to Wikipedia this demeaning term was particularly used by German Jews towards Eastern European Jews.)

Charles, my grandfather, was definitely the head of the household. Rumor has it that he would sit at the dinner table with a whip at his side, lashing out at those who did not adhere to family rules. Unfortunately, my father received the brunt of his criticism and wrath. But Charles had different sides to his personality. He could be a harsh parent who appeared to be cruel at times, but on the other side was a strong family member who had supported his eleven brothers and sisters whenever they needed help. (They all lived nearby.) He was a big sweets eater, and could often be found at the nearest bakery while taking breaks from his police duties.

Dad had two sisters and Bertha (Bertie) was the favorite and always the life of the party. She would sing and play jazz on their baby grand piano whenever company came, encouraging everyone to sing along. Sister Beatrice had a different role within the household. She was born with a club foot, resulting in a significant limp. It embarrassed her parents to have a disabled child, and they intentionally kept her at home and out of sight. Years later they had her committed to an institution. According to Mom, Beatrice was mentally fit and was only minimally impaired, and no way deserved to be "put away" as she was. Mom visited her once she said, but the rest of the family never did. Reportedly, they never saw her again.

It was such a difficult environment for her to live in, and Mom felt strongly that they had to get out of her in-laws' home as soon as they could save enough money for first month's rent deposit. Dad's Aunt Anna came to the rescue. She owned an apartment building on the Grand Concourse and had a place for them. They moved in in 1928 to a bright and lovely two-room space with a step-down living room. It faced the concourse. Dad was working as a taxi driver at the time while Mom worked in a millinery store.

In January 1929 she gave birth to my sister Millicent (later called Penny) and gave up her job to stay home with her. With only one income, they struggled to pay the rent. Aunt Anna offered them a smaller apartment in the back of the building.

"It was quite a letdown—dark and cold," Mom remembered. But somehow, they managed. The Great Depression hit that October when the stock market crashed. That was the end of the taxi cab business for Dad, as people could barely put food on their table, few were out in the streets hailing cabs. So they moved again. This time to live with my maternal grandparents, Ida and Pasa. Though they had only a small two-bedroom apartment on Tremont Avenue, they still welcomed Mom and Dad in.

Chapter 4
Billy

BILLY WAS BORN IN 1932. Somehow, they were able to find a more affordable apartment around the corner and Grandma Ida looked after the children while Mom and Dad worked.

Then in 1936 there was a recession. That winter Mom got the idea from a friend to go to Florida and open a bar there. Florida was the new frontier she was told—like the old California Gold Rush. It was where you could make money, hand over fist. She had the drive, the ambition. Quick decisions came easily to her. Dad went along with the idea at first, so they packed up Billy and Penny and moved south. Dad was to tend the bar while Mom took care of Billy and Penny and made sandwiches to sell at the bar. They were huge—specially made for the many construction workers in the area—turkey and roast beef on rye with a mound of lettuce on top of sliced tomato and Swiss cheese, finished with a horseradish dressing. They sold well. But there was a major glitch to their overall plan: it wasn't really what Dad wanted to do. He was a quiet man, and a teetotaler to boot—a man who had never had a drink in his life. So being a bartender didn't come naturally to him, and according to Mom, he didn't put much effort into it. It lasted six months—the place flopped, and Mom blamed Dad.

"He never was the earner I wanted him to be," she told me years later. More than once she told me in a bitter tone, "I was the main breadwinner in the family."

In frustration and anger, she left with Penny and Billy to return to New York. Dad was to remain in Florida until he could sell the bar.

Back in the Bronx, Grandma Ida wasn't well enough to care for Penny and Billy, so finding a suitable babysitter for my brother and sister became a problem. No one they knew was able to help out. Scrolling through the newspaper, Mom came across an ad posted by a Mrs. Alice Webster, who boarded children. She had a large house in the country where children could stay during the week, according to the ad. Mom took a trip up to find out if it would be suitable and safe for Billy and Penny and was impressed with the environment. Each child would have a comfortable room adjacent to one another. There was a swing set in the backyard for them to enjoy. Mom took a liking to Mrs. Webster. She would watch the kids, feed them, and keep them safe, she promised. Her own children were already grown. The only disturbing thing to Mom was the lake on the property. It was quite a walk from the house, but it still concerned Mom.

"I don't want the children near the water," she told Mrs. Webster repeatedly.

"Definitely not," Mrs. Webster concurred. However, another woman was staying at the house with her baby and one very hot day she took the kids for a walk to the lake. "I'll take care of them," she said to Mrs. Webster, who was preparing dinner for the night.

"Please, can I go in the water?" asked Billy as they came upon the lake. "Please! It's so hot."

"I guess it would be all right, just to get your feet wet," the woman replied as she helped him slip off his sandals.

"No!" eight-year-old Penny said insistently. "My brother is not supposed to go into the lake. Don't let him go in. My mother doesn't want us to go in the lake."

As the woman didn't know that there was a big drop in the bottom of the lake, she paid no heed to the little girl who was protesting. After just a couple of steps in, Billy slipped under the surface and there was no way to get him out.

I can only imagine the telephone call Mrs. Webster made to Mom, and Mom's frantic reaction. The police had to drain the lake to find her five-year-old son's body. It upsets me just to think about it and to even have to put it into words. As I was not born yet, of course I never knew Billy, but I can feel empathy for their pain and the loss that they all must have felt.

Dad, of course immediately, returned to New York. The family went into mourning, but they didn't mourn together. Mom, I was told, could barely get out of bed. Meanwhile Dad blamed Mom.

"Why did she have to send the children away?" he continued to ask, although I doubt if he ever asked her that directly. Eight-year-old Penny had seen her brother drown right before her eyes. Yet no one seemed to recognize the trauma she had gone through.

"No one comforted or paid attention to me," she vividly remembered many years later. Not her parents, her maternal or paternal grandparents, or anyone else, she recalled.

It had a great impact upon her and affected her profoundly for the rest of her life! I believe it had a significant influence on the relationship between Penny and Mom, and caused a lot of conflict over the years. Once a year had passed, their family doctor said to Mom, "Why don't you have another child?" And she did. That child was me.

Chapter 5
I Arrive

OF COURSE, MY BIRTH DIDN'T magically solve all their problems. After losing Billy, Mom lost all her belief in religion. We didn't have Passover Seders or celebrate Chanukah like most Jewish families did. We never went to Temple. My father didn't object as he hadn't had much of a religious upbringing. Any mention of religious events brought out the ire in Mom until eventually, it brought her into Atheism.

I was born in the Bronx right around the corner from Ida and Pasa who lived on Tremont Avenue. Aunt Berdie, my father's sister, her husband Arthur, and their sons lived just down the block. It was a wonderful support system. But Mom was still concerned about the rent. She had heard that Brooklyn was cheaper, so when I was three years old, we moved to Bensonhurst into the top floor of a two-family home. It was much larger than our tiny Bronx place. We made good friends with the Gross family—who had two daughters—who lived downstairs. As a young child I didn't have any difficulty with the change of environment, but as a fourteen-year-old, my sister missed her grandparents, her friends, and her cousin Jimmy, who she was very close with. She remembered the very long lonely walk she had to take to Seth Low Junior High School by herself. In the beginning it wasn't easy for her to make friends at her new school. Eventually, of course she did meet some nice girlfriends, and then later, a boyfriend. He was a little older and very aggressive. Ultimately Penny became pregnant. Mom and she went out of town until she gave birth. The baby, a little girl, was adopted by one of the nurses at the hospital. I was too young to be aware, but I know that this was undoubtedly a very emotional and difficult time for Penny. It became a closed topic—no one spoke of it. Then, fifty years later, Ellie, Penny's daughter, began to search for and found my mother. She and her own daughter, Jordana, came into New York and that's where we all met one another.

We continued living in Bensonhurst as I made my way through elementary school. I became a member of the Brownies, proudly wearing my uniform. Dad began to tutor me in multiplication as I got to the upper grades. Every evening we would go over the times tables. He would persist until I had learned them very well.

Although Dad had worked as a subway conductor when we lived in the Bronx, he eventually changed his position to become a New York City Transit bus driver when we moved to Brooklyn. Every day at lunch time he would bring the bus home and park it directly in front of our house, right on the corner of 80th Street and 20th Avenue. I never knew if this was legal or if he had permission to do so, but we all found it amusing to watch him pull up at almost exactly the same time daily. We made a habit of standing by the picture window, giggling. "Dad's home for lunch!" one of us would say. I remember him having the same lunch every day: four soft-boiled eggs and four slices of white toast which he laid out directly on the table. He was a man of habits!

Although Dad worked locally, Mom took work wherever she could get it, and I missed having her at home. I often thought about going to see her. It felt to me like she was always working, and as a young girl I often waited, glued to our Brooklyn window, peering out to see her to return home. So one Saturday, I made the decision to travel to her work. For just a quarter I was able to take the train to Coney Island. I was eleven years old; I walked to 18th Avenue, took the long flight of stairs to the El, and got on the subway. I remember that the seats were made of woven rattan that left a crisscrossed pattern imprinted on the back of my legs.

I found the store easily. There she was, sitting in the window, stitching a hat. Her eyes opened wide in surprise when she saw me walk up to the door.

"How did you get here? And how did you find the store?" she asked, looking startled.

"You took me here once," I said, "and I remembered where it was."

She smiled, and I thought she seemed pleased that I had gotten there on my own.

It was her friend Alice Canfield's shop in which Mom had rented the window. Alice sold dresses and as always, Mom specialized in millinery.

I stayed with them until they closed and we took the train back home. The store was on a side street because the rent was cheaper but unfortunately it didn't draw enough people and so the dress shop went out of business before the year ended. Of course, that meant the end the millinery sales, too.

Mom wasn't able to find another job in millinery. But then a friend told her about an opening for a job in the city. That's when she first began working as an usherette in a Broadway theater. She worked in the evenings, showing people to their seats, and came home late at night. It was then that she got her IATSE union card which came in handy many years later.

My father was expected to be home in the evenings while she was at work, to keep an eye on me. But he rarely was. Often, I would awake during the night, feeling lonely and scared. We lived in a two-family house in Brooklyn at the time. We were on the 2nd floor and still living above our close friends, the Gross family. Using a large wooden spoon, I would bang on the kitchen radiator to get Sonny Gross's attention. Eventually she would come to the bottom of the stairs. Looking up patiently, she would ask, "What's wrong, Cora?"

"Do you know where my father is?"

"He just went to get the newspaper," she would reply. "He'll be back soon." But he wasn't. Thinking back upon it now, he was most likely downstairs with the neighbors, but he didn't want to encourage my dependence on him. He always felt that my mother tended to pamper me, and in his view, I was old enough to stay in the apartment by myself.

Since we lived in Bensonhurst at the time, Mom had to take an hour-long trip to get to the theater. Eventually, she got tired of the long ride and she moved on to different work. Over the years she held down many jobs.

"I was always the main breadwinner," she explained once again. Dad worked regularly, either as a subway conductor or a bus driver. But I suppose the pay wasn't high. And according to Mom, it was not enough to make ends meet.

I remember her being a Fuller Brush salesman, selling home cleaning items door to door. I think she might have been the only Fuller Brush woman, at the time.

The Fred Astaire dance studio was several blocks from our apartment. It was on the street where the overhead train ran. Mom became a dance instructor there, specializing in the rhumba.

At home, she taught my father and me how to do the box step. "Side together back, side together front."

To the tunes of Tito Puente, she instructed, "Quick, quick, slow—back together forward," she repeated until we got it right

Being a young teenager, her lessons provided me with my first introduction to dance. I took to it easily, especially anything with a Latin flavor, which I still love to this day.

A few years later, she had the opportunity to become an assistant buyer. It was the late 1950s, when women typically stayed at home once they were married and had children.

"Your mother is different. She goes to business, not like the other mothers in the neighborhood," my friend Eileen commented.

And she did. All dressed up in her wool suits and fashionable hats, she had entered into a new lifestyle. Her friend Gertie who was a clothing buyer in Manhattan had asked Mom to be her assistant. Gertie was a demanding woman who put my mother through the wringer by making her work long hours without providing any recognition for her efforts. She also stood in the way of Mom's moving up and progressing. I remember when Mom used to come home from work tired and stressed out with headaches that would keep her in bed for the rest of the night. It upset me to see her this way. I would take a washcloth from the linen closet, hold it under the cold running water, wring it out, and place it on her forehead.

"That feels nice and cool," she would comment each time I did it.

Finally, the Sampson buying company they worked for recognized Mom's abilities and promoted her to full buyer. She enjoyed working with the clients. It reduced her stress level as she felt fully in charge of her own abilities. Somehow, there were no more headaches.

"I'm selling the house," said our landlady one day. "The new owners will be here in a month and you will need to pack up and leave before then." She delivered this without a hint of emotion.

It was my turn to be uprooted. This time Mom found an apartment in a three-family house owned by a doctor and located in Boro Park, Brooklyn. I'm not sure if my atheistic mother realized that it was adjacent to a very orthodox Jewish section. As a matter of fact, 46th Street, our new street, was the border line between Orthodox and less observant Jews. It remained that way as long as we lived there, but in later years the entire area became Ultra Orthodox, including Hasidim and other sects. (Currently is it considered one of the primary Ultra Orthodox areas in New York City.)

I was almost thirteen years old when we moved to our new home on a hot August day. My parents were at work, and I didn't know a soul. I spent most of my time sitting on the front steps outside the house, just waiting and feeling lonely. Dad was selling vacuum cleaners at the time and Mom was still employed at the Sampson buying office.

Finally in September, school opened, and I became a student at Montauk Junior High School. Luckily I quickly made some new friends. It was a wonderful time for me. One of the delights of our neighborhood was 13th Avenue, our main shopping street. It was filled with food stores, clothing shops, and much more. People came to shop there from various parts of Brooklyn. You could stop at one of the bakeries for a charlotte rouse (a soft cake topped by whip cream and a cherry). The rouse came wrapped in a circle of cardboard which could be pushed up from the bottom. Pickle bins sat outside the delicatessens, where you could choose a sour or half sour to munch on as you walked the avenue. At the southern end of the street there was a chicken slaughterhouse. This is where the orthodox Jews bought their chicken every Friday afternoon for Shabos.

Our little group remained together through high school and beyond. We hung out at the local candy store with all the other neighborhood kids. It was just harmless fun, listening to the jukebox, sipping an egg-cream, possibly meeting a potential boyfriend.

After I finished high school, I got a job in the Sears buying office on West 32nd Street off of 8th Avenue. Mom drove us both into the city every morning.

"I'm so excited," Mom told dad and me one night after work. "I've been invited to go into business with two of the other buyers from Sampson's."

"How's that going to work?" Dad asked with quite a bit of skepticism.

"There are going to be three different departments, one for each of us. I met with them for lunch today. They've thought it all out and it sounds good. We are going to start looking for offices tomorrow." It didn't take long before they found something suitable.

"It's going to be perfect!" Mom told us. "Just the right size for the three of us and a small waiting room in the front. However, it's not available yet. We have to wait till the other tenant's lease expires, which is in a few weeks." Meanwhile, the women all gave their notice at the Sampson office and they began to contact some of their clients to tell them of their potential move. Mom went shopping for some new business suits. Then she settled in until their new business could open.

"I have something to tell you," Mom said as we sat at the kitchen table with a cup of coffee. "What is it?" I asked her.

"I've decided to go on a vacation to Europe in July. It's a long trip—five weeks and five different countries."

"Wow. Really?" I replied.

"Yes. It's a good time to do it now." It was a surprise, but I guess I was never shocked by Mom's adventures.

"Instead of flying, I'm going across by ship."

Mom booked our travel on the S.S. United States.

"Is Dad going?" I asked, even though I knew her answer would be no.

"No, I'm going by myself."

Thoughts of it played on my mind. I was so enthralled by the idea. I couldn't wait till the morning to ask if I could go with her.

"I don't know. It's a very costly trip."

"I have some money in my savings account at the Emigrant Bank—my inheritance from Grandma. Remember? I can use that to help pay my way."

"Well, that will cover part of it. I'll think about it." A couple of agonizingly long days later, she said, "Yes, you can come."

"Thank you, thank you!" I said as I jumped into the air.

I was going on nineteen and had recently broken up with a boyfriend. In truth, he broke up with me. After six months he said he wanted it to end.

He was older and more worldly. On our first date he took me to see *Carmen*. It was my first opera. But I guess I no longer fit into his lifestyle. He told me this when he dropped me off at the door on our last night together.

"None of my friends like you," he said, rather coldly. It was such a shock to me, coming out of the blue like that. I cried so loud and gasped so much, as I walked up the steps to our apartment, that everyone probably heard me. Not just my family but the neighbors downstairs, too. Totally crushed, I had moped around the house for weeks. I avoided going to work, too.

My parents and my sister tried to console me, but I couldn't seem to get past it. It was my first big heartache. Therefore, the idea of a trip overseas gave me something new to plan for and think about. It was such an exciting idea! I have always suspected that Mom had planned this trip as a ruse to help me get out of my funk. But she wouldn't admit it.

We were just working people, not particularly well off, but I never thought about how this trip was funded. Not until many years later did I learn that Mom had taken a loan from the bank to cover the cost. Notably, she did the same to finance many of her travels.

Chapter 6
First Trip

SO A FEW WEEKS LATER, we walked up the gangplank onto the *S.S. United States*. As was the custom back then, people came to see us off. It was standing room only as fifty people drank champagne in our stateroom—family, friends, and Mom's business associates joined us. We stood on the deck as we waved farewell to our visitors as the ship slowly began to depart from port.

There were three classes on the ship and we were in tourist. We shared our room with four complete strangers. The cabin had three sets of bunk beds. I took the top of ours. One of our roommates was a young woman with a strong German accent. As a Jewish woman, just the fact that we were rooming with a German person was upsetting to Mom.

Memories of the Holocaust and the horrors which came with it caused mother, as well as so many other Jewish people of the time, to be mistrustful of and angry at all Germans, regardless of whether or not they had had any involvement in the war.

It wasn't too difficult for Greta to pick up on Mom's coolness and the way she averted her eyes when they passed.

"Are you angry with me?" she asked one morning. After she assured us that she was too young to have been a part of the horror, and that she totally abhorred it, peace came to our room.

The S.S. *United States* held the record as the fastest ship to cross the Atlantic in 1958. It took three and a half days. We were both seasick the first day until our bodies became adjusted to the motion.

Although our stateroom was tourist class, we dined in luxury. More than we had ever seen. Musicians serenaded us with their violins as we partook of the best wine and gourmet cuisine. We were so excited when we finally arrived in Port of Le Havre and then took the train to London.

The changing of the guards, Hyde Park, Trafalgar Square, English breakfast, high tea, and Indian curry for dinner. We loved it all. On our third night we wanted something more familiar and we decided upon Chinese food. Our hotel concierge highly recommended Wo Hop.

We walked into the very large restaurant and turned to look at one another. Yes, it was Chinese, but not at all like Chun King located on Flatbush Avenue in Brooklyn, where we went every other Sunday for egg foo young or lobster Cantonese.

Upon entry we could hear the big band and see its leader waving the baton. He was dressed in a white dinner jacket. Waiters scurried to serve the tables surrounding the oval-shaped dance floor. There was additional seating available at the top of a large open circular staircase, where we took our seats.

As I swayed in my chair to the beats, a man who looked to be in his early twenties approached our table. His hair was a sandy shade of blond and his eyes a soft blue, and he wore a grey tweed jacket and a knitted tie.

"You seem to be really enjoying the music," he said, smiling. "Would you like to dance?"

It seemed perfectly natural to me that he asked, and I loved to dance, so I replied.

"Okay. Yes. I'd like to." As we walked downstairs towards the dance floor, the maître d' came running up the stairs.

"No dancing!" he said, "—not with someone you didn't come in with." Both of us were startled by his reaction. So we invited John to join us at our table to which he gladly complied. We found out he was from Scotland, visiting friends in London. We got to know and like him quickly. He was easy to talk with and so down to earth. After dinner he asked us if we'd like to go to a late-night jazz club. I remember it was located in a cavernous basement and everything on the menu was dirt cheap. But the jazz was good. He was with us every day from then on and stayed at our hotel for our last night in London. There was definitely a strong attraction between us. We stayed at an economical hotel with the bathroom down the hall. While my mother left the room to get ready for bed, he took the opportunity to become amorous. Her return knock provided as an interruption of our lovemaking. Otherwise, we might have gone "all the way" as they used to say back in the day.

The next morning, we all went to Victoria Station to catch our train to Amsterdam, which was planned as our next destination by our travel agent back in the states.

"If you had stayed in London a few days longer," John told me, "I probably would want to marry you."

I liked him, but it was all such a whirlwind. At that point in my life, I just decided to move on, never knowing or saying anything to encourage him. My mother, however, gave him our home address and asked him to write.

The next morning, we stepped off our plane in Amsterdam—such a fascinating city. A reservation had been made at the Grand Hotel Krasnapolsky in the center of Dam Square. People on bicycles surrounded us—men and women going to work, others with children riding along with them; even the elderly preferred this mode of transportation. We quickly had to learn how to stay out of their way so as not get run over.

Our only complaints were that Mom's beer was always warm and they had no ice to put into my Coca-Cola. We took a canal ride to Edam where the cheese was made and bought some to take home. The thick red wax covering of the rounds made them safe to transport, we thought. The sky opened up after the tour and we were caught in a torrential rain. We stood under the eaves of someone's home, waiting for it to stop.

"Why won't someone invite us in?" mother inquired, as we heard the click of the lock at their front doors. The Dutch did not strike her as the friendliest of people.

Next we were on to Zurich where we spent hours shopping for an Omega watch. We rode the cable car up Mount Pilatus overlooking the beautiful city of Lucerne.

Mom left her brand new expensive camera on the tram that was mailed back to us weeks later by the people who ran the tram. Luckily, she had left her name and address in the camera case. It was quite a surprise for us, the New York skeptics we were, to receive it. We thought we'd never get it back. It was gone forever in our minds.

The luxurious Hotel des Balances was where we spent our time in Lucerne. It was built in the twelfth century in the shape of a chalet, right on the river so guests have a beautiful view. We felt very pampered to be rooming there.

Our last stop in Switzerland was Lugano. We stayed in the Italian-speaking section of the city which was an elegant relaxing place. As we sat by the water, eating ice cream from a street vendor, Mom said, "I haven't had ice cream this good since I was a little girl in Russia. *Morozyvo*, that's how you say ice cream in Russian."

"*Morozyvo*, is that how you say it?" I tried to repeat it.

"Not exactly," she replied.

The next morning, we were off to Italy. The train ride was an experience. A middle-aged Italian woman, hair pulled back into a bun, sat diagonally across from us. She tried to converse with us, but since neither Mom nor I spoke Italian, we couldn't answer her. When that didn't fly she asked, *"Français?"*

"Oui, un peu," I responded.

My high school French, along with a lot of hand flailing and pantomiming, came in handy that day. We were having a nice chat until the train stopped and the *Polizia* came charging on. They entered our car and asked to see everyone's passports. Afterward they went rifling through the overhead luggage compartment, confiscating cigarette cartons, which belonged to another cabin mate. It seemed like he had some explaining to do, but ultimately no charges were made against him. The whole event was a bit frightening, but it passed quickly and we proceeded to Rome.

There was so much history and art and religion to see in that amazing city. We had time to experience much of it, as we spent more time in Italy than any other country. The people we met there were the most friendly of any place we visited.

That included handsome Antonio, the young man who came to our table every day at breakfast; I really don't remember how this came about. Maybe Mom arranged it to cheer me up. (I wouldn't put it past her.) But by that time, I didn't need any cheering. Maybe he thought we were wealthy Americans even though we were staying in a *pensione*, which was far less expensive or fancy than a hotel. We couldn't talk to each other because neither spoke the other's language.

One day, a newlywed couple sat at our table. We watched the wife feed her husband green grapes, picking them off the stems and placing them in his mouth. I thought it was cute and did the same for Antonio, amused and laughing the whole time.

Another day he asked me to go for a ride on his motorcycle. Someone in the hotel translated for me.

"He said to tell you he's going to see his lawyer, and would like you to take a ride with him?"

I got on the back of his Vespa and held on tight as he drove through the city. Mom never made an objection. It was a safer time back then. When we got there, I waited outside. It didn't take long and he took me directly back to our hotel. The whole thing was a mystery. I had no idea why he went there or what he was doing. On our last day, he gave me a photo of himself in which he was posed like a model.

I still have his picture.

We covered so much of Italy, loving every bit of it, from the north to the south. Our last stops were Capri and Anna Capri, where we had to duck our heads as we took a canal ride through the Blue Grotto.

Next was France—the final country on our tour.

We would have had to take three trains to get to Nice: from Sorrento to Naples, Naples to Rome, Rome to Nice. Instead, we decided to fly.

Nice provided us with a different pace. It was a resort city. Each day we walked along the promenade adjoining the sea. In the evenings we ventured into town for dinner. One day we took an early morning bus to charming Monte Carlo. Everything there was quite expensive. Mom denied herself her typical morning coffee because it would have cost her $5.00

for a cup—not an unbelievable price today, but astronomical back then.

One day, I got tired of Mom's gift shopping, so I sat on one end of a bench by the water while I finished up some postcards. A man sat down on the other end. He had pitch black hair and a thick mustache.

"Hello," he said. "You must be from the states. You look like an American."

"Yes, I am," I answered politely.

"What part?"

"From New York—actually Brooklyn. Where are you from? Are you French?" I asked doubtfully.

"I am from Algeria."

"Where is that?"

"We are a country in Africa," he said, explaining some of the history of his country. "Did you never hear of us? Right now, we are fighting for our independence from France."

"Oh! But you live here?"

"I live here and I work here so I can send money back to my family in Algiers."

"That's nice. Where do you work?"

"At Air France. At the reservation desk. Can I ask you something?"

"Yes," I nodded and he came right out with it.

"I'd like to go to bed with you—will you?"

"No," I replied, for some reason, not shocked. Actually, I was a tiny bit flattered.

"How old are you?" he pressed.

"Nineteen," I foolishly answered.

"Are you a virgin?"

"Yes," I answered, once again, foolishly.

"You are nineteen," he commented with surprise, "and still a virgin?" When I didn't respond, he said, "I have to go back to work, my lunch time is over. Here is my card. Call me if you decide to change your mind." I took the card and said nothing in response.

Two days later, Mom was on the phone, frantically trying to get a reservation to Paris. We would be returning home from there.

"The only thing I can get will bring us back to the ship on time, but with absolutely no chance for sightseeing!" she said. It was August and all the Parisians were returning home from their summer *vacances*. It was the city she was most anxious to see to observe the women of Paris in their fashionable clothing, to walk down the Champs-Élysées, to taste the cuisine and wines. She was disappointed, and I felt badly for her.

"Remember the man I met who works for Air France?" I said. "Would you like me to call him? I think I still have his card."

"Yes, call him." And so I did.

"Hello—do you remember me? You met me sitting on the bench, by the water."

"I remember you."

"I'm calling because my mother and I are having trouble getting a flight to Paris. I was wondering if you would be able to help us?"

"Yes, I can help you," he said.

"Oh good," I said.

"On one condition: if you go to bed with me," he replied. I smiled and hung up the phone. We never did get to Paris. Not on that trip anyway.

Although mom didn't get to see Paris that trip, she made up for it for by visiting many times over the years. She loved the food, the bistros, and the brasseries. She even learned a few phrases in French. The flea markets provided another attraction for her. That's where she often found the antique jewelry which she could sell back in New York. The city of Nice was another love of hers; she became quite familiar with the hotels and derived great pleasure from just walking around the city, exploring the shops and restaurants. Mom continued to travel, well into her nineties, visiting various parts of Europe and Asia. This nine-year-old little immigrant girl from Russia with barely any schooling ultimately became a sophisticated traveler. One could say that she "was a woman of the world."

Chapter 7
Family Travel

MOM PLANNED TRIPS WITH OTHER family members as well. She especially liked taking her grandchildren on various adventures and trips. However, it didn't always work out as she had intended.

Andrew, my sister Penny's younger son, said, "I remember it so clearly. I was just five years old when Grandma took me to the New York City Heliport and we climbed into a copter. I did not like it at all. I had no idea what was going to happen and I already had a fear of heights. My parents got really upset with Grandma because she didn't ask if it was okay to take me on the copter. Although it was meant to be fun and exciting, the whole 'adventure' left a bad taste for everyone involved."

At twelve years old, Mitchell, who is Andrew's older brother, was at a better age for travel. Mom decided to take him to Mexico. He vividly remembers every detail of the trip.

"First, we went to Mexico City and stayed at a shabby hotel until we could move on to something more upscale. While we were there, Grandma took me to a bullfight. It was wild and crazy to watch the bull being stabbed to death right before our eyes.

Then afterwards we went out for a steak dinner. I've often wondered—could that have been the same bull?

"Acapulco was our next stop. I remember that our flight got cancelled, so instead Grandma hired a driver to take us out for an eight-to-ten-hour drive. On the way, we stopped for lunch on a 'bizarre riverboat' that the driver had recommended. Once we arrived in Acapulco we checked into a fancy Hilton Hotel. It had a great circular pool with multiple bridges. I loved swimming and jumping off those bridges. It was super fun for me. Grandma sat by the pool, constantly watching me because there was no lifeguard. But since I was a good swimmer, there was no problem.

"It was little more dangerous when she took me swimming at the beach where there were huge rocks in the water. It felt like body surfing in the ocean and sometimes I got slammed onto the sand. Good thing I was a strong swimmer, so I never got hurt. And I loved it."

My daughter Alison was eleven when one summer, Penny and her second husband, Charlie, came for a New York visit. Mom thought it would be fun if all of us could spend the day at the Bronx Zoo. My family lived out in Suffolk County, Long Island at the time, and would have to take the Long Island Railroad in.

"Come into the city and we can take the train up," she suggested to me. The problem was my hesitation to travel in the city. It was the early 1980s, the city was in bad shape, and I thought it was dangerous for my young children. At the time, New York City Transit was notoriously unsafe. Well, Mom to the rescue. She decided to hire a limousine so we could see the animals. There were probably other options, but Mom didn't wait around to make decisions, she just ran with her ideas and didn't let much stand in her way. Soon we were off in the black limo to see the gorillas and giraffes.

Mom took another trip with Alison when she got a little older. They flew to Florida to meet Penny and then journeyed to Sanibel Island. Penny loved going to this barrier island, located on the Gulf of Mexico. She and Charlie often rented an apartment there so that he could fish and Penny could look for the shells that covered the beach. It was a special place. So this time, Mom, Alison, and Penny went together for a weekend.

"All day we walked the beach, finding interesting-looking shells and filling up our baskets with them. When the sun began going down, we gathered them up and brought them back to our room. After we ate dinner, we sorted through them to look for the prettiest ones so Aunt Penny could use them to make necklaces. It was a lot of fun. Aunt Penny told me that she would sell the jewelry at different art fairs around Florida," Alison recalled.

Alison, Aunt Penny, and Mom also took another trip together. As Mom loved visiting France, she wanted to introduce Alison to that same experience—for her sixteenth birthday.

They traveled to Nice, one of Mom's favorite places, and also to Cannes. Mom took them to her favorite hotel that she always stayed in in Nice and they settled there. They all enjoyed seeing the sights on the promenade and sampling the wonderful restaurants. "For lunch we would sit on a bench in the park, sharing a big baguette spread with French butter and sliced cheese. It was like a picnic," Alison told me.

On the final day they stayed in a hotel in Cannes. "It was very fancy with lots of wealthy people. Everything was good until Grandma and Aunt Penny had an argument—Grandma had made a new friend and asked her to join us, and I think Aunt Penny was mad about that. She and Grandma stopped talking to each other. I didn't know what to do and hated it because I felt in the middle." When I think back now, I realize how difficult it was for Alison. *What could she have done, with feelings of loyalty and love for both of them?* I ask myself as I write this.

Mom and my son, Brian, had many trips together. They went to a family wedding in Annapolis, Maryland at the Naval Academy and also toured Washington D.C., although Brian barely remembers the wedding. The next year, they went to Montréal via Amtrak.

"I really had fun in the city but the train ride going there was terrible. We didn't like how smoky it was and it was also very late. So Grandma got us on a flight home," Brian told me. Later, when they were both a little older, he became a good travel companion for her. They went to Paris in 1994, when Mom was ninety years old. "Brian didn't spend all the time with me," Mom told me later on. "But we always met for dinner and went to a nice restaurant."

"I did some exploring around the city on my own," Brian told me. "Grandma was able to navigate fine. She knew all the buses and could find her away around, because she had been there so many times over the years. She did fine."

Enjoying it so much, Mom continued traveling well into her nineties. I had told Mom about my exciting vacation in New Mexico. My husband and I took lots of photos of the beautiful scenery, including those of the characteristic Pueblo architecture. Looking at the pictures became an inspiration for Mom to venture there. Almost immediately, she planned a trip to the area, combined with a visit to my sister, Penny, and her son, Mitch, who each had homes in Phoenix, Arizona. A few weeks later, she and Brian flew out there to spend a few days. Next it was on to Albuquerque, where they rented a car and Brian drove them to Santa Fe. On their first night there, Mom began to experience breathing problems. They departed quickly for the nearest emergency room.

"It's the altitude," Doctor Santos told her. "I'm certain that's what is causing your respiratory difficulty. Its over 7,000 feet here in Santa Fe, a huge change from New York City which is only 33 feet above sea level. It's not unusual; I see lots of out-of-town visitors who have the same reaction."

"What do you suggest I do, Doctor?"

"Return home. You seem to be in general good health, but at your age it is the safest thing do."

"Go home?" Mom said. "I just got here, we haven't seen anything yet, and I paid all that money to get here. I don't want to leave. Is there anything else I can do to stay here for a few days at least?"

"Well, I could put you on oxygen, if you insist—we can see if that helps you," replied Dr. Santos.

"Good idea," Mom said. And so they stayed. With the assistance of an oxygen tank at night and a portable machine during the day, they completed their trip.

Chapter 8
CGR Is Born

WHILE MANY TYPICAL WOMEN OF the 1950s were expected to stay at home, caring for children and husbands, three gutsy ambitious ladies who thought differently used the initials of their last names and opened an office in the prestigious Penn Plaza building at 200 West 34th Street.

The triumvirate consisted of Annie C, a busty, brash, bleached blond who bought the dresses, Gloria G. an elite, refined woman with a touch of snobbishness who purchased ladies' sportswear, and Fran R. (Mom—you must know her by now) who bought sleepwear and lingerie. Their office was a large square with an attached conference room and a small waiting area. There were three large desks—Annie's in the center, so she could hold court.

The salesmen from the manufacturing companies often waited up front for an opportunity to show her their new dresses. Annie was completely comfortable in her role, always wheeling and dealing to get the best prices. Nobody was going to put one over on her.

Jack, her husband, was also in the "shmata" business, as a manufacturer, so she knew all the ins and outs. Maybe that's what made her such a natural.

CGR opened with a bang. They had customers who owned small stores throughout the US and Puerto Rico—some of whom they had brought with them from the previous office where they worked. I don't think it was unusual at the time for people to "steal" clients from another office by promising them something they weren't already getting.

Store buyers and owners came into New York City regularly to see the latest fashions and to purchase clothing from the manufacturers. When a retailer couldn't get into New York, the buyers would act as their eyes and make purchases on their behalf.

The 1950s fashion was all about hats. Hats were a necessity for the well-dressed woman or man to wear: men and women sported them into business, they wore them on the subways, the fashionable ladies of CGR wore them all day at work. Annie's were mostly large brimmed, and often in red. Gloria, being more subdued, wore a grey or beige pillbox. (The hat made famous by Jackie Kennedy.) I especially remember her husband, Bernie, showing up in his homburg every day when he picked her up after work. (He impressed me as the much more relaxed of the two, always having a good word to say.) Mom tended towards the bucket cloche, which was a tall hat, worn low on the head to frame the face.

The CGR ladies were knowledgeable about the

market and would escort clients to various showrooms within the garment district in the West 30s. I believe they got commissions from the manufactures, and also payment from the clients.

They hired me to work in the office when they realized they needed a receptionist and secretary. The timing was good for me because I had lost my job at Sears—after I took my five-week, unapproved vacation to Europe.

I got married in 1960 and moved in with my husband Ira to an apartment in Forest Hills, Queens. Unknown to me, my moving out gave Mom her long-awaited opportunity to leave my dad: after thirty-eight years of marriage, she could leave, knowing I was married and settled.

They hadn't been compatible for many years. Still, my father was shocked. Dad knew that Mom wasn't happy and that their relationship wasn't the best. He would have had to have been blind not to see it. But I don't think he ever thought Mom would take such a drastic step.

He was a quiet man and I doubt that the two of them ever had a conversation about their marital problems. Oh, Mom expressed her anger and frustration quite frequently and they both held resentment toward one another. I remember a lot of yelling and anger from Mom towards Dad.

"Where will I live when you leave? This is too expensive and too big for just me," Dad said. "I'll help you find a place," she answered. They did—a few blocks away in an older apartment building, with a bedroom and combination kitchen-living room. Dad took the two black-lacquered cabinets with the painted gold handles (that he had built to Mom's precise specifications many years ago) with him. They became bookends to the sofa that he also took to his new place.

Mom was ready to embark upon a new chapter. Once she helped my father get settled she moved into the city, signing a lease for a lovely studio in a new building on West 34th Street. It was perfect, so conveniently close to her office. It brought her pleasure to be back in Manhattan where she had spent her formative years.

Their separation surprised me even though I knew she hadn't been happy with Dad. Still, I never thought she would go through with it. Since I was married and no longer living with my parents, it didn't affect my day-to-day life. Mom was thriving, but it was sad to see my father alone and forlorn. Our holiday celebrations were never the same after that. We had two separate birthday parties when my son Brian turned one. Mom came to one, and Dad to the other.

Once in her fifties, Mom began to experience some health issues. She was diagnosed with high blood pressure and was put on medication. She remained on the medication all her years. She took it regularly and there were never any negative effects from her hypertension. It was also in her fifties was when she had her first surgery. Because she was having sinus problems, her ear, nose, and throat doctor advised her that she had a deviated septum. He suggested that surgery could help alleviate her discomfort.

She wanted to correct it, but also to have what was then called a "nose job" because she had inherited her family nose, with a bit of a hook. She was admitted to the hospital the day before and a friend went to see her.

"Fran, you look wonderful. They did a terrific job on your nose," said Ginny, to which Mom replied, "Thank you, but they haven't operated yet." Her nose did look great once the procedure was completed. It was petite and a perfect fit for her face and no more hook. Years later her grandchildren (my son and daughter) were looking at some old photos when they asked in surprise, "Is that a picture of Grandma? Her nose looks so different!"

"Yes," I responded. "I guess you didn't know she had nose job."

CGR had been in business for several years when Mom's two partners Annie and Gloria came to the decision that they weren't making enough money. They forced Mom out of the company, claiming she wasn't bringing in enough business. Her department did bring in less, because lingerie and sleepwear were not purchased as often as outerwear. Let's face it, most women would prefer to buy a new dress rather than a new pair of pajamas. At first, the partners offered Mom the option of taking a reduced income.

"Half a loaf is better than none," Annie proposed. But Mom refused the offer. It was a very difficult and emotional time for her. She was angry and was very hurt at the same time. Also, she needed an income. One of her ways of dealing with it was by listening to the music of Herb Alpert & The Tijuana Brass on vinyl. She played their LPs over and over to keep her mind from dwelling on her troubling situation and to cheer herself up.

"How can they do that?" a woman named Helen asked. "Don't you have a contract?" They were sitting at the diner on 8th Avenue at separate but adjacent tables and they had started a conversation. Helen was complaining about the long hours at her job, which gave Mom the opportunity to talk about her problem at CGR, where her partners were trying to push her out of the business. It was almost dark when they realized other customers were coming in for dinner.

"What's your phone number?" Helen asked. "I enjoyed talking with you. Also, I'd like to know how things work out for you."

"I'll write it down for you," Mom replied as she handed her the paper napkin she had written it on.

I guess Mom got motivated to continue because before long she opened her own buying office by taking some of CGR's clients with her. She also sued her partners for breaking their contract and happily, she won the case. During this whole time period I worried about her. Her new office was small and dark, and I didn't know how she was faring, or if she had enough money.

"Remember, I won the suit, and I got a substantial settlement. I'm doing all right," she told me, to quiet my concern. Still, I could see the strain on her face and I wasn't convinced.

She kept her stresses to herself, never sharing them with me, at least, or with most others I suspect. I think it's what instilled in me the belief that she was Superwoman, a woman to greatly admire. It turned me into the number one member of her fan club.

As it happened, it was really too difficult for her to earn enough in the small company to keep herself going. She needed to make a change.

Ultimately, she closed her office and got a job as a buyer for Askin, a large national chain with headquarters located on West 32nd Street. For several years, she remained there. It was a good company to work for and she got along well with her boss. But having a regular job was never enough for her. She was the original multitasker, always having a side business. As a lover of antique jewelry, she had developed quite a collection, purchasing pieces mostly at the various NYC flea markets. She became such an enthusiast that she decided to sell the pieces herself. While still working full time at Askin, she began to look for opportunities to market her jewelry. Often it would be in the window of a store.

There was a record store on West 34th Street that caught her imagination. They sold collectable records and had an empty bay window that she thought would be perfect to display her wares. One day she approached the store owner, asking if she could rent out their window. One, two, three, and he agreed. It would put more money in his pocket, *so why not?* he thought.

It was a dusty unkempt place, sort of a dump. Their one and only salesman slept on a mattress each night in the back of the store. None of this bothered her, as she could see the potential. She set up a beautiful window display and attracted lots of customers. An electric coffee pot was always plugged in at a side table, lending a fresh-brewed aroma and for Mom and her customers to enjoy a cup. The bay window at the record store window turned into one of her most successful business endeavors. Some of her regular customers became long-term friends.

"We met in the elevator of our building," Jade told me when I inquired how she had met my mother. "I was only twenty-one years old, and your mom was such an interesting-looking, well-dressed older woman. I had a feeling we could be friends. We said 'hello' and the next day I saw her in the shop window, displaying her costume jewelry. When I stopped in, I saw that the pieces were circa 1930s and 1940s—my favorite styles—but I was just starting work as a model and actress, so I didn't have much money to purchase anything. One time she asked me to watch the 'shop' because she had an important appointment. I sold a couple of pieces while she was away, which I was happy to do. Sometimes she and I would just sit and chat between customers. I loved hearing her stories about her life experiences. She told me about the time she had gone to the Paris flea market to scout out jewelry, and had bought some nice pieces. She was excited to bring them back to New York to sell—or planned to. But then she left her satchel with them in the taxi."

Once Jade's career took off, she got a big part in *The Last Emperor*, which was filmed mostly in Beijing, China. "The movie was a huge success and won a lot of awards," she told me. "I made sure that Fran and I kept in touch through the years. She invited me to all her birthday parties as she got older, and I practically felt like a member of the family."

Another business venture in Mom's life wasn't quite as successful. She said, "I had a partner in a shop on 9th Avenue. Derek was his name. He was kind of a dumb guy whose boyfriend Zack had set him up with the store to keep him busy. It was empty when I got there and I stopped in to look at it. There was an antique sign out front, but no antiques. When I met Derek, he said I could put some furniture in there just to fill the place up with merchandise, so I did. It was my old couch and some of my friends added their discarded furniture, too. Zack's friends added other furniture and knickknacks to the inventory. When everything sold out quickly, I decided to put my costume jewelry there.

Derek was not really interested in selling and became easily bored with the idea. Every day, Derek waited for Zack to call him from Europe, where he was traveling for work. Once he got the call, he'd go across the street to hang out with his friend. One of those times was when the robbery happened. The thieves broke through the beautiful old etched front door by cutting a hole in the glass and took the cash register and all my jewelry. There wasn't any insurance, so I didn't get reimbursed and I don't know what happened to Derek after that. I never saw him again."

Continuing at Askin Stores until 70 years of age, she decided it was time to retire. But within a short time of leaving, she became restless and wanted something part-time to keep her busy and to bring some extra money in.

Remembering back to the time years ago when she had worked as an usher at a Broadway theater made her think about renewing that career. She had saved her union card from twenty years prior, which she found at the bottom of her desk drawer. Saving this card was a lucky move, enabling her to get a job at the Uris Theater on West 51st Street. She worked the matinees and evening performances. Like all the other ushers, she wore all black except for the white Peter Pan collars, which were required. Later on, the

Uris had its name changed to the Gershwin Theater in honor of George Gershwin. It was and still is one of the largest Broadway houses, accommodating many well-known musicals.

One of the perks of her job was the ability to get comp tickets, which she generously gave to the family. When she couldn't get comps, she sometimes bought us tickets for shows she felt we shouldn't miss. The first show I remember seeing was *The King and I*, starring Yul Brenner.

My son, daughter and I went to see it. There were no comps this time because it was selling out. At first, the three of us sat on the theater steps until one of the other ushers located three empty seats for us. Today this could never happen there is no sitting on stairs and comp tickets are rare. But in those days, the rules were much looser. We also saw *Pirates of Penzance*, where Kevin Kline came on stage as the swashbuckling pirate. Estelle Parsons and Linda Ronstadt played leading roles as well. *Starlight Express* opened in London, then later moved to the Gershwin. With music by Andrew Lloyd Webber combining R&B, rock and roll, jazz, and country western, it was the first show to be performed entirely on roller skates. It was based on Rusty the steam train, a character in a children's story. The cast included Andrea McArdle and Jane Krakowski. We enjoyed it, but the play had many critics of this unorthodox new-fangled show. It did become a success around the world, as it was seen by over twenty million people and grossed twelve billion dollars. Some other great shows which Mom worked were *Camelot, Porgy and Bess, My Fair Lady, Annie* and the ghoulish *Sweeney Todd*, which has a new production this year. I remember seeing many of those , thanks to Mom. Mom's "temporary" job lasted much longer than expected. She worked as an usher in the orchestra of the Gershwin, escorting patrons swiftly up and down the aisles to their seats for the next twenty years until she reached the age of ninety. She told me then she was ready to stop.

They made her a big party when she left, and were totally taken back by her age, because she had never told anyone at work. Martha, the chief usher, arranged the party, inviting all the other ushers to attend, as well as Scott, their manager.

Mom decided to get a divorce. She wanted to take the next step and make her separation with Dad permanent and legal. In the mid-20th century, many Americans traveled to Mexico to obtain a "Mexican Divorce." A divorce in Mexico was easier, quicker, and less expensive than a divorce in most of the US. Many celebrities obtained a Mexican divorce, including Johnny Carson, Katherine Hepburn, Elizabeth Taylor (when she divorced Eddie Fisher), Marilyn Monroe (from Arthur Miller), Jayne Mansfield (from Mickey Hargitay), and more. It was often referred to as a quickie divorce, a "fast-track" process in contrast to American divorce procedures which involved additional bureaucracy and more expense. Many US citizens utilized these divorces until 1970, when Mexico began to limit them. Also at the time, the United States began to offer alternative reasons to divorce your spouse. And so, Mexico was the place to go if you wanted a reasonably priced divorce at the time when Mom decided to go ahead with one. Also, she wouldn't have to pay for an attorney.

The Honorable Rodolfo Silvan, clerk of the First Civil Court, Bravos District, State of Chihuahua, Republic of Mexico, presided and made the judgment as follows: Ciudad Juarez, Chihuahua, Mexico, July 3, 1964. Whereas to finally resolve the suit for necessary divorce. Reasons given: incompatibility of temperament and having not cohabited together for some time.

As a result she received a COPIA CERTIFICADA DE SENTENCIA DE DIVORCIO from:

PODEF JUDICIAL DEL ESTADA, CHIHUAHUA.

This further upset and disappointed my father, but I think he was resigned to it by this point. He and I never had a real discussion about what was occurring. He attempted to bring it up one time, but I felt so awkward and I didn't really know what to say. Of course, I knew how unhappy my mother was and I guess Dad sounded so unexpectedly surprised by her actions. Sometimes when you are living in a situation, even an unhappy one, you just think it will go on forever. But I did understand how hurt he must have been, and the difficulty he had with this enormous life change.

"Did you know that Fran is divorcing Dave?" asked Millie, Mom's old friend. Her question had an accusatory tone, almost as if it were my fault. Having met Mom as a young girl, Millie, and her husband Jerry, had remained friends with both Mom and Dad for over fifty years.

"Yes, I know." Was the only response I could offer. I felt so caught in the middle and so off guard—particularly since my father was standing right next to us.

Mom, on the other hand, felt relieved. It was the end of an era for her, a new beginning. She had settled into her work schedule, and was happy to have the ability to walk to work from her apartment. It was a happy time in her life. Her little studio faced east and had good sun in the morning. Before work each day, she would put her plants outside the double windows on her fire escape. When she arrived home one evening, she immediately noticed that one plant had been knocked over onto her living room floor. Before venturing further into the apartment, she dialed the super.

"Has anyone been in my apartment today?"

"No, not at all. Why are you asking?" Right then a man ran from the bathroom shower, grabbed her purse and ran down the stairs. Instinctively Mom ran after him, shouting, "Give me my pocketbook!" There was no way she could catch him—he was too fast and got away with her driver's license, money, and whatever else was in her bag.

She was a strong woman, but this shook her up tremendously. Of course, anyone would feel this way. My husband and I went to see her to try to offer some support. But she no longer felt comfortable staying in her apartment and began to spend nights at a good friend's place who lived down in Greenwich Village. I guess I believed by going to see her and offering my support that I could help her deal with the situation. In hindsight, I realize now how naive and futile my intervention was to her. I was only in my twenties, but still, I wonder why I didn't take it more seriously. I ask myself now, was it because Mom downplayed her feelings? Was it because I didn't want to feel her pain? Was I in denial? Or was it because she had always exhibited great strength whenever encountering a problem that faced her? To me, she had always been Superwoman. Shortly after it happened, Mom learned that a neighbor in her building also had experienced a break in. Only hers was different. The intruder had remained in the woman's apartment, raping her repeatedly. Mom wanted out! Anyone would have felt exactly the same way.

"I need to get out of here—to find a new apartment," she lamented. By that time, Mom and Helen had become good friends.

"Come stay with me for awhile," she offered. Mom, who had always been independent but was too afraid to remain in the apartment after the incident, accepted Helen's invitation to sleep on the sofa bed in her tiny apartment in Greenwich village. Meanwhile, she asked around to find another apartment in her neighborhood.

She found one quickly—across the street at the intersection of 34th Street and Dyer Avenue. It was a large pre-war building, antique looking with a certain charm about it. There was an old-style elevator run by an operator. I can still picture Jimmy with his blue blazer jacket, always with a smile, riding people up and down. Also, 433 had no fire escapes, which made Mom feel more relaxed. It was a much smaller place, but had high ceilings with a large window facing 34th Street. Most importantly, it was much safer and provided Mom with a feeling of security. She remained in that building until moving to Manhattan Plaza, many years later.

As she entered her late seventies, she began having trouble walking.

"I can walk a few feet but then I have to stop for a bit before my leg begins to hurt," she told me over the phone. When I went into the city to see her I was shocked because I was so accustomed to watching this agile woman flit about—she looked more fragile then I had ever seen. After the testing, her doctor found that the artery in her leg was blocked. Off we went to see Dr. Papodopilus, a vascular surgeon at Brooklyn Hospital. He had been highly recommended by her physician. Not only was her leg blocked but the doctor also found blockage in both her carotid arteries. These very important arteries run up and down the neck, bringing blood to the brain. Her right artery was 80 percent blocked and the left, 90 percent which significantly limited her blood flow. Dr. Papodopilus scheduled her for surgery wherein they would remove an artery from her groin to repair her left leg. It greatly improved her ability to walk without pain.

"The next procedure we will do is your carotid artery. We only need to do your left side. Let's arrange an appointment in six weeks."

"When you do the surgery Doctor, would you be able to do a little neck lift at the same time?" Mom asked with a teasing smile on her face.

"Sure," he replied with a chuckle. Surprise surprise, *I think he really did it*. Not only did her walking improve after the surgery, but her neckline looked much tighter, particularly on her left side. Arthritic pain seems to come to us all as we age. Instead of complaining about it, Mom found her own remedies. Tiger Balm ointment was her main go to. It came in little, tiny, round tins, which she would buy in Chinatown and massage into painful areas of her body. Ace bandages also helped. I can still picture her strategically wrapping one around her arm or leg, to control pain. Later on, the doctor recommended Tylenol Arthritis, a more traditional treatment.

More surgeries followed during the next years. In her eighties, she had cataract surgery in both eyes. It went well with no hitch and she was happy to ditch the glasses she had worn for many years. In her nineties, she had two hernia operations—the second was to correct the first. However, she never adjusted to the discomfort of the mesh that was placed in her abdomen during the operation. "I can feel it inside me all the time!" she told me, annoyance in her voice.

Chapter 9
Birthday Parties

PARTIES COULD BE FUN AND of course Mom knew this, so periodically she threw one for herself— she had an intentional reason for doing so.

"I don't want any gifts. It's not really about celebrating my age. I'm just trying to keep the family together," she explained before the first event.

Mom did not physically embrace us—she didn't hug people when they came to visit or kiss them goodbye when they were leaving. But she did embrace the people in her life by trying to keep them close.

Every Sunday, the entire family would go to see my grandparents in their Bronx apartment. But after my grandfather passed, followed quickly by my grandmother, family gatherings became infrequent. Everyone was busy with their own lives. Mom was the one who decided to put in the effort to keep the family connected. She hoped that we all could maintain closer relationships. This was her rationale for throwing her own birthday parties. Becoming sixty-five seemed to her to be a momentous age, so that was the first party she held. Not only were her siblings invited, but also nieces and nephews and their children. My husband and I went with our six-month-old son, Brian, still with a headful of curls because we put off cutting it, wanting him to keep that baby look. Everyone was delighted with the chance to see him for the first time.

That sixty-fifth party was held at a hotel near 14th Street. At the time, Mom was working in the buying office from Monday to Friday, but on the weekends she also sold collectible jewelry. She had a small cubbyhole-like spot at an indoor flea market across the street from the hotel. Always the multi-tasker, she would also make sandwiches in the morning, which she then sold to the other vendors. Like a lot of entrepreneurs, she saw a need and filled it. A thermos full of hot coffee was also included and welcomed—after all, in those years, Starbucks was not on every corner. As an immigrant from Russia, she had begun to work at fourteen years old. I think working hard became part of her DNA.

The party was a huge success—the whole family came: my sister, her husband and two sons, my aunts and uncles, my cousins and their children. Some of Mom's old friends were invited as well. We had a great time; we laughed and got to visit with relatives we hadn't seen for ages.

Marchi's restaurant, on East 31st Street, was selected as the destination for her next party—her seventy-eighth. Marchi's served prix fixe meals and was known for its special pastry. Since the 1930s they had served the same Northern Italian five-course dinner. (Unfortunately, they closed their doors in 2019 after their eightieth year.)

Mom found it to be a charming, different type of place and hoped her guests would enjoy the experience. I got to see cousins whom I hadn't seen for years—probably not since the last party. At the end of the meal, the waiters carried out Marchi's specialty in large trays held overhead. The trays held high mounds of crispy crostoli, a feathery-light dessert— their house recipe.

For her eighty-fifth birthday, Mom pulled out all the stops and her friends and family all gathered in her studio apartment for cocktails and conversation. She greeted us wearing a knee-length black leather skirt that she had recently purchased in Spain, paired with a white silk blouse.

"I hired one of the actors who lives on my floor to be the bartender," she told me, when we spoke on the phone before the party. "And he's gorgeous," she had added.

The tall, thin bartender was dressed in a tux. He served us drinks from behind a card table, set up in the corner of the living room. Guests mingled and leaned on the kitchen counters while catching up with one another. Who had a new grandchild? Who had just started college? Afterwards, we piled into our cars to head down to Chinatown. Mom had hired two limos for those who didn't have transportation.

We arrived for dinner at the dim sum restaurant on a small side street, even though dim sum was traditionally eaten in the morning or early afternoon, as Mom had specially arranged it for us. We placed ourselves at three long narrow tables; large tea urns lined the back wall and a very Chinese tiramisu sheet cake with raspberry filling served as our dessert.

A few years later, when she reached ninety, she felt ready to retire from her position as an usher. The head usher made her a party inviting all the other ushers. She had been there almost twenty years, escorting theater goers up and down the orchestra aisle to their seats. The other ushers were surprised to learn her age, as she had never told anyone.

Once she retired, she had more free time. One of the places she enjoyed visiting was the Chelsea Market on 19th Street. It was very easy for her to travel there on the bus.

Their green market inside the Chelsea Market was a favorite and she went there almost every week to buy her vegetables. Upon exiting the store one day, she slipped and fell. Immediately the owner and staff came running to her aid. They insisted upon calling the emergency crew.

"How are you?"

"Are you in pain?"

"I'm okay—no need for me to go," she repeated. But they were concerned for her well-being and had her taken to the nearest hospital.

"She had a hairline fracture of the pelvis, the doctor told us. He kept her in the hospital a few days and then sent her home to receive physical therapy. That's when she began to use a cane.

She hated the cane at first until a friend told her, "It makes you look so distinguished, Fran. Mom made the best of it and never placed blame for her injuries. The shop owner kept in touch, checking up on her. A friendship was created as a result of the accident. Joe and his wife invited mom to the various cooking shows that were being filmed upstairs in the studios at the market.

A few months later, they learned that her ninety-third birthday was coming up soon. The owner of the Chelsea Market suggested that they throw her a party. It was held in a large room used for special events. Many of the the small vendors in the market provided food; the Thai restaurant, one of the Italian bistros, and several bakeries contributed. She was a

Ninety-three years old

regular and they all had noticed her. "Invite all your friends," they told her. "As many people as you like."

Quite a cast of characters came, those she knew from many different walks of life. There were five different birthday cakes in all. The invitation read:

HATS OFF TO FRAN.
NO GIFTS, but everyone please wear a hat.

And so they did. Guests arrived in straw cowboys, felt derbies, Russian furs, and French berets to name a few.

Chapter 10

One Hundred Years

I INSISTED UPON A CELEBRATION of her one hundredth year.

We had it at Le Madeleine, a well-known French Bistro right across the street from her apartment on West 43rd Street. It was another of her favorite haunts.

French food was her favorite. She had learned to enjoy it on her many trips to Paris.

"What are you going to wear to your party?" I asked her.

"I'm going to wear all my pearls," she answered. She looked so glamorous, decked out in her chokers and her long white strands. A red velvet hat and a tapestry handbag complemented her black outfit.

Close family members and friends were all invited. Three employees from Amy's Bread also came, bringing with them a beautiful chocolate devil's food cake as their gift.

Mom was a regular at Amy's; even at the age of one hundred years, she was still able to walk up to their store on West 47th street to enjoy a cup of coffee and a piece of cake—but when she arrived at the shop, it was for far more than just a piece of cake.

It was for a visit!

"Fran's here," the counter employees would call out whenever she entered the bakery. Then all came to welcome her, especially the manager, who became one of Mom's biggest fans. She was so popular and so admired that they included her picture and a story about her in their latest cookbook, entitled *The Sweeter Side of Amy's Bread: Cakes, Cookies, Bars, Pastries, and More from New York City's Favorite Bakery.*

They describe her in the book as "a neighborhood legend. A woman who had lived in New York during the Roaring Twenties and the Great Depression. But she doesn't live in the past. As a modern NYC woman, she is up-to-date on world events, politics, and fashion trends."

At the book-signing party in their Chelsea Market store, where people asked for Amy's autograph, some also asked Mom to sign the page of her story.

A short time later, Amy went on *The Martha Stewart Show* to promote her new book. Mom was invited to be in the audience and I accompanied her. She sipped coffee as we waited in the green room. We had our hair done, then went to a rehearsal.

During the show, Martha Stewart pointed out Mom in the audience.

"One of Amy's favorite customers is in the audience and she is one hundred years old."

"Wave, Mom," I said, when Martha pointed her out.

100TH YEAR BIRTHDAY

Chapter 11

More Health

AFTER HER FALL AT AGE ninety-two while in the Chelsea Market, Mom began to use a cane—her walker came several years later. One of her neighbors offered Mom her old, motorized wheelchair because she was getting a newer model. Mom tried to drive it and she expected me to help her with it. I attempted to teach her but was afraid she might fall using it in the street, particularly while crossing. We made it up to the elevator and that was about as far as we got.

"I wonder if we can get someone more expert to teach you?" I thought aloud. But we couldn't find anyone who could or would. She had been looking forward to carousing the neighborhood in her chair, but it just sat in the corner of the living room, collecting dust.

Until she reached one hundred and four, she was doing great. Around then, she became too tired to walk outside—once again shocking me because I was convinced that she would go on forever, as she always had. Of course, that wasn't reality based, but she just seemed unstoppable. We arranged for a physical therapist to order a wheelchair for her. It was measured and designed precisely for her petite size. But she didn't want me to wheel her around, thinking she was placing a burden upon me. However, I was happy to do it.

"Mom, I'd rather push you in the wheelchair so you can get wherever you would like to go." Once she had accepted my offer, she began to enjoy the ride, and our outings became a positive time of the day. She was able to find joy in it. She wasn't one who worried about the future, she lived each day as it came. I don't remember her expressing any fears of getting older. Although she did once say, "I'm curious about reaching one hundred. I can't help wondering: what will it be like for me?" But, neither did she dwell much about the past. "I have no regrets," she once shared. She lived in the moment. I guess you could say she was a practitioner of mindfulness before mindfulness became a popular philosophy of modern culture.

As I sat outside The Little Pie Company recently, enjoying a slice of their famous peach, Carole, a Manhattan Plaza resident, walked by. She took a seat at my table and I told her I was writing about Mom and asked her for some of her memories of Mom over the years.

"I used to see Fran at the Good and Plenty food shop when they had tables outside. She was in her nineties then," Carole told me. "Every day she came downstairs using her walker and always wearing a hat. We would usually sit together for a chat. She was delightful to talk to and ready to greet you. She was not a smiley person. She was real person. Very real! I found it unusual for someone her age to take such good care of herself. She always looked well put together, never slovenly or unkempt. She was also an interesting role model for lots of people in the building. People knew how old she was, and we all had a great deal of respect for her. Nobody messed with her. If you did, she would put you in your place—always in a subtle way of course! Being a Sagittarian, as I am, she was open for conversation. We tell it like it is and don't hold back. Once Fran made up her mind, she just went ahead and took whatever action she had to. I found her to be very disciplined and to know how to handle things.

"I was always curious to hear about the places she had traveled. She also talked a lot about certain French restaurants in the city that she liked. I think one of them was Les Halles where the now-famous Anthony Bordain was the chef.

"Lots of times she would be off on her rolling walker, going to catch a bus. 'You are going on the bus with that?' I asked her once. 'Sure, it's not a problem. I just get in the back door which has a lift,' she replied. 'This is what I live for: to be able to get out every day and go somewhere else different,' she told me with excitement."

Mom continued to travel into her nineties, visiting various parts of Europe and Asia.

Chapter 12

Puerto Rico

IN HER NINETY-EIGHTH YEAR SHE had grown tired of a very cold New York winter. One of her friends in her building had a friend who owned an apartment in Puerto Rico. Mom communicated with this woman by mail and arranged to rent the apartment for a week. She invited her grandson, my son Brian, to fly down with her, but he couldn't get away due to work responsibilities.

The apartment was a large place with two bedrooms and two baths. I was worried about her going alone, and suggested that I go with her.

"Okay," she said, "but I'm not paying for your fare."

"That's fine. I wasn't expecting you to. But if I come along, will the apartment cost you any more?" It would not.

The apartment was on a prime street in San Juan. A series of steps greeted us at the front entrance—no ramp and no handicapped entry. The building super escorted us through the side entrance that went through the basement, where they kept the garbage cans. We took the elevator to the third floor in order to enter through the outdoor patio. The patio was fenced with a gate with a combination lock.

Mom's friend-of-her-friend, Rebecca, had left a long list of instructions written on a yellow legal pad, including

1. Be sure you lock the gate at all times.
2. Do not open the windows on the south side as thieves frequently climb up the building to commit robberies.

On and on the list went. Mom thought I was overly cautious when I paid heed to the instructions. She was relaxed and wanted to have a good time. Mom got upset when I offered to carry her walker down the front steps instead of taking the elevator through the creepy basement. She tried to walk the walker down herself but almost fell, so I carried it for her as she walked down, holding onto the banister. I guess her annoyance with me was increasing. She was an independent woman who didn't want to be "coddled." Almost every day we took the shuttle bus down to old San Juan. We shopped and lunched to our hearts' content. One morning while waiting for the bus, I suggested she hold her purse over her other shoulder so it would be easier for her to manage—she lost it.

"I don't need anyone telling me what to do!" she retorted. I was hurt by her remarks, and she knew it because I barely spoke to her after that.

That night as we were both getting ready for bed, she offered me money. "If you need money, I can give you $10,000," she said. Her impetus for saying this was most likely due to my occasional complaints that my husband tended to be somewhat frugal.

"I don't need any money," I responded. I didn't want it, nor did I need it, and I knew that $10,000 was half of all the money she had in the world. Nevertheless, it was an extremely generous offer. Of course, this was her way of breaking the ice! I didn't take the money, but her offer helped me get over my anger. It made me realize just how desperate she was for us to get along.

When I thought about it years later, I realized that she would have been fine on her own. The apartment owner had made all the arrangements to assist her. The building super had been put on call to help her. The shuttle-bus driver would have assisted her with her walker. She knew how to be charming—she could charm your socks off if she wanted to. She knew how to ask for help if she needed it. She was a world traveler. She wanted and needed to maintain her independence.

Chapter 13
Politics

"I ONCE WAS A MEMBER of the Communist Party," Mom told me one day. "I always had an interest in politics, even in my early years," she added.

I wasn't surprised to know this because she had always made her opinions well known. Her reactions were strong and vocal in regard to both those she admired and those she did not.

But she wasn't alone in joining the party as many of those emigrating from Russia at that time had strong socialist and labor union values. As a matter of fact, her brother Jack was very involved in the formation of one of the labor unions in the garment industry.

The Communist Party USA was formed in 1919. People like my mother, who held socialist beliefs, decided to join it—this wasn't unusual during the Great Depression when there was widespread sentiment that capitalism had failed. Shortly after its founding, there were 60,000 members. At the time, the party concentrated on helping to build labor unions and improving workers' rights. It lobbied for higher wages, a national retirement program, and unemployment insurance.

I don't know exactly when she joined the party or how long she remained a member. It may have been later on during the Great Depression when the party offered a hopeful outlook to the masses of unemployed Americans workers. She and my father were struggling just like everyone else during that time. (There was never any mention of my father being involved in the party.)

During World War II, the Communist party grew to 75,000 members. Then in 1945, a wave of anti-communism swept America. Senator Joseph McCarthy and the House Un-American Activities Committee went on the attack of those they believed were members of the party.

One of Mom's first political heroes was President Franklin Roosevelt. FDR became a great liberal icon of those same Eastern-European Jews who believed in socialist values. Although years later, he was thought to be anti-Semitic, at the time, the country was not aware of this claim. His New Deal policies provided the benefits that they had hoped to achieve—social security and unemployment insurance. And so, they continued to worship him as he brought many Jewish Americans into the Democratic Party. Mom and Dad remained devoted Democrats throughout their lifetimes and Mom donated as much as she could to those running for office.

I found an autographed picture in her desk of President John F. Kennedy with his brothers, Robert and Ted. It says, "Dear Fran, Thank you for your support of the Democratic Party." She had saved this photo for forty years, because it meant so much to her. Equally, she admired President Bill Clinton and his achievements in office. His sexual dalliances didn't perturb her at all and didn't affect her high regard of him as a President.

Not only was she democratic, but she was a liberal as well, subscribing to and enjoying reading articles in politically progressive magazines, such as *Mother Jones* and *The Nation*. I often saw her sitting at her kitchen table by the windows, engrossed in an article from one of these publications. Afterwards, she liked to read them to me so we could discuss them.

The Iraq War was extremely disturbing to her and she was highly against the administration responsible for initiating it. It made her so angry that she talked about it nonstop whenever the opportunity arose. In 2006, the war had been ongoing for three years, and at the time she had reached the ripe old age of one hundred and two. One day, she fell in her apartment and the Emergency Department responded to her call. As mentioned, this wasn't the first time she had fallen. The paramedics checked her out and she seemed to be physically fine.

Mom at the celebration of her 103rd birthday at Manhattan Plaza.

"We need to take you to the Emergency Room," they told her. "Just to be sure you are ok."

"But I don't need to go to the Emergency Room," she said. "I'm fine and nothing hurts."

In an attempt to check on her mental status, they decided to ask her some questions:

"How old did you say you are?"

"One hundred and two. I was born in 1904."

"What city do you live in?"

"New York City."

"Who is the current President of the United States?"

"That BASTARD, George Bush!" she vehemently replied.

Looking at one another, the paramedics laughed and said, "Lady, you are doing okay. You don't have to go to the ER after all."

Chapter 14

Just Another Day with Mom in NYC

IT WAS A BRISK WINTER day and Mom wanted to get some air. She was a hundred and three years old and still lived by herself in Manhattan Plaza. Since I had recently gotten an apartment in the building, we were able to spend many of our afternoons together.

The weather didn't faze her. It never deterred her from doing what she wanted to do. When it was cold, she would wrap herself in a scarf. If it rained, she would put her plastic bonnet atop whatever hat she was wearing that day.

One day, she decided to go to one of her favorite places to shop, the International Grocery Store on 9th Avenue, to replenish her coffee supplies.

Putting on her long black leather coat, she slowly and deliberately attached the oversized buttons and fastened the snap at her neck. Her hats were all around her, encased in large, round, flowered boxes stacked on the floor. Others were placed upon stands that sat atop her dresser. She chose a champagne-colored silk and tilted it on her head at just the right angle. I thought to myself that it was kind of summery, but I didn't comment. It looked so pretty, and she seemed so satisfied with it when she glanced in the mirror.

On went her dark sunglasses. They made her look elegant and even a little bit mysterious. But in actuality, she wore them to keep her eyes from tearing up due to the outside elements.

Slowly, she pushed her big-wheeled Rollater walker from our apartment building on West 43rd Street, all the way to West 40th Street. We passed the 99 Cent Fresh Pizza stand, where people buy a slice and eat it as they stand on the sidewalk.

Across the street from the Port Authority, we encountered a group of homeless men, sitting on the concrete floor. They gathered there to wait for the van which delivers free food every day. An elderly black man noticed Mom.

"Hi, Grandma. How are you today?" he asked. Mom nodded and said, "I'm okay. How are you?" Mom judged no one. We continued slowly to the grocery store. We could smell the pungent odors as we entered the shop. It was filled with open barrels and bins of exotic spices and coffee beans. On the counter sat jars of multi-colored olives. The large refrigerator held all sorts of Greek cheeses: feta, kefalotir, and manouri. Mom was greeted warmly as soon as she walked through the door. The owner, a man with a thick black mustache, welcomed her. An elderly lady sitting on a chair in the back of the store waved, saying, "Look at us! We are both still here." Mom waved back with a smile.

"What would you like today?" the counter clerk asked.

"I'd like a pound of coffee, half mocha java and half Columbian, mixed together," she requested. They ground the coffee for us while we waited and put it into a small brown paper bag. After our purchase, we made our way back to our apartments, stopping first at The Big Apple store to buy a semolina loaf—a delicious golden-colored bread topped with sesame seeds. It's hard to buy just one, but we knew we could come back tomorrow for another. As we waited for the traffic light on the corner, a woman excitedly approached us, wide-eyed.

"Are you the woman whose picture is in *The Sweeter Side of Amy's Bread* cookbook?" she asked Mom. I nodded yes because I wasn't sure that Mom could hear her.

"We saw you on *The Martha Stewart Show*! It was when Amy was talking about her book. I remember that Martha introduced you while you were sitting in the audience. She told everyone that you were over one hundred years old and one of Amy's favorite customers. My mother and I were watching the show together, and we were so impressed by you. I'm so happy to have the chance to meet you," she said. We both thanked her.

"That's so nice of you to say," I replied.

As she walked away, I could hear her on her cell phone. "Mom! You will never guess who I just saw!" Funny how Mom used to call me, saying the exact same thing.

Close to home we stopped at the fruit cart. The vendor was a Pakistani man who had been there for years and knew everyone in the neighborhood. I never saw him when he wasn't smiling. "Hi, Mama," he said to her.

"I only need one banana," she said in reply. He put two or three in a bag.

"No charge," he said. It was just another typical day with Mom on the streets of New York.

Chapter 15

Later Years

MOM MANAGED MOSTLY ON HER own. She remained living in her Manhattan apartment until she was one hundred and four years of age, maintaining her independence because she liked it that way. Mentioned earlier, one of her favorite restaurants, La Madeleine, was a well-known French bistro directly across the street. When no one was available to join her, she would head over there by herself for dinner. They treated her royally—a glass of champagne came with every meal. But Mom couldn't always drink it all.

"Would you like to take the rest home?" the waiter would ask.

"Yes, that would be nice," she'd reply, and the hostess would proceed to put the remainder into a takeout cup. When she was ready to leave, she'd help Mom button up her coat and escort her back to the building. Later, Mom would sip her drink while watching TV.

As she progressed through that one hundred and fourth year, things began to change. Mom decided that she could use some help. She contacted an agency that assigned an aide, Tureka, to assist with grocery shopping, showering, and cleaning. Mom actually only wanted help with showering but that wasn't available by itself, so she signed up for the minimum of three days a week, four hours a day. When I suggested that I could help her shower, she replied, "That's not for you to do." There really wasn't that much for Tureka to do to fill those weekly hours. It irritated Mom greatly that she'd spend a good deal of the time just sitting on a chair, swinging her leg to and fro.

Mom lived on the 7th floor and I lived—and still do—on the 20th. I usually went down to her apartment to warm up her dinner that was usually purchased from the takeout shop called Good and Plenty. In the afternoons, we would take a walk to fulfill Mom's daily request: "Let's stop for a cup of coffee." Most days we went to The Little Pie company which was right down the block. We couldn't miss the sign, EAT FRESH PIE, that was stenciled clearly on the glass front door of the tiny shop. Even if you missed the sign, you'd be enveloped in the wafting smell of apples baking in their warm crusts. The Little Pie Company was originated by a resident of our building, Arnold, who used to bake pies in his 4th floor apartment, sometimes he'd even borrow neighbors' ovens so he could produce the right quantity, before opening his store.

Mom took her place at the table by the front window, parking her walker to the side so she was able to see whoever was walking by—sometimes she waved back at neighbors.

On a high energy day, Mom would decide to walk the four long blocks to Amy's Bread on West 47th Street. There was a large step up to enter. She could manage that, but waited for an employee to lift her walker over the stair. This Hell's Kitchen store is in a 1925 building with a large picture window at its front.

"Sit down, Fran. We'll get your coffee with a slice of devil's food cake," Keri, the manager would say as she stopped to chat. The baker, Francesco, invariably greeted her with enthusiasm. He loved to see her, although she never got his name right, always calling him Fernando. There was no need to walk back home as the 9th Avenue bus #11 brought us directly there.

Late in the day, she'd tune into *Judge Judy*. Wow, did she enjoy it. She would sit right up close to her small TV set so she wouldn't miss a thing.

"I like the way she solves the problems, and decides the cases," she would tell me.

As the years passed, she began to lose her hearing. She had hearing aids but struggled with them and lost her patience with the batteries, so she gave up using them. Finally, her vision had also became a problem. She had macular degeneration, but I didn't know it at the time, since she went to all her doctor's appointments alone, before I had moved into the city. Mom had been getting care for years at The University Eye Center, College of Optometry, located on 42nd Street. I went with her a couple of times and they gave very thorough exams. At the time, her eyesight was fine. First the interns or residents would check her out, then the doctor would come in. When I realized how much her vision was failing, I contacted them, but Mom had never signed a release form allowing family members to be advised of her health needs. I don't think it was her intention to hide information. She probably didn't think it was necessary. Nevertheless, the social worker advised me of her condition.

I'm not sure Mom understood the significance of it when her doctor told her she had macular degeneration, but as it worsened, she could no longer read her beloved magazine articles, or even watch her favorite show. No more *Judge Judy*.

"I'm not for this world anymore," she began saying frequently. "I'd like to die, but I don't know how," she said as the time moved on. That's what she related to me, but no one else would have guessed that she felt that way. Mom had a front face for the world to see. Always displaying a smile and a positive remark, even when it wasn't how she was actually feeling.

She'd had several falls during the previous few years.

"I wonder why I never break anything?" she'd say. "Maybe it's because I'm so close to the ground?" pondered my four-foot-six mom.

In the fall of 2009, in her one hundred and fourth year, Mom fell in her kitchen.

"I was just standing at the kitchen counter, eating a piece of cake, and I fell," she told me as I stood looking down at her. "I wasn't even doing anything."

A few minutes earlier, I had gotten the call from her Lifeline alarm system. After I rushed to her apartment, I found her neighbor, Tillie, next to her. Mom was lying facedown on the kitchen floor with one arm under her head. Tillie had heard Mom's calls for help, and had a key to open her door. The Emergency Technicians were already on their way, and Mom was asking for a pillow for her under her head.

Tillie said to me, "It's your call, Cora. I didn't want to move her."

"I think it's ok to slip one under her head," I said, grabbing a pillow from her couch. Just then the techs arrived and swiftly put her on the gurney. I rode with her to the ER at Roosevelt Hospital on 10th Avenue.

Much that happened after that is a blur. Once she was admitted to a hospital room, an orthopedic surgeon came in to see her to tell her she had broken her hip.

"We are going to operate tomorrow morning," he said. I was quite taken by surprise.

"Do you think it's okay to operate on a woman of her age?"

"Yes! And if I don't operate, she will never be able to walk again!"

The surgery, at least, went well. Mom was started on recovery immediately. The nurses sat her up in a wheelchair with a pillow behind her. She did well. The next step was going to rehabilitation. Now the tough decision came. I had to think of her well-being after the rehab because I didn't know if she would be able to return home again. The hospital social worker, Sharon Kapolsky, gave me a choice of rehab/nursing facilities. After I visited two or three rehab places, I chose the Amsterdam House on Amsterdam Avenue at 100th Street. It was highly rated as the best in NYC. I also wanted a place on the west side of town that I could get to quickly and easily in order to be there with her as much as possible. It wasn't right next door, but I could easily take a bus up there. Apparently, it was a desirable place but they did have an opening.

They started her physical therapy right away and she did well. She could walk fine holding onto the railing—which she did proudly, a big smile displayed on her face—in the therapy room. They kept her in a wheelchair the rest of the time. She, along with the other patients, sat around the nurses' station, doing nothing for most of the day.

They put large bolsters on the sides of the bed so she couldn't get out of bed. Although they did that to prevent her from falling, I still wasn't happy that it was another loss of control for her. I asked many times for them to remove them, but they never would, because they were so short staffed. This also meant they didn't always have an aide to accompany her to the bathroom—so she had to wait. I knew all this was frustrating her terribly. She complained each time I saw her. It frustrated me as well. So I suggested that I hire her aide from home to be with her. This was permitted by Amsterdam House.

"You can't help me, and neither can she," she spat out at me when I made the suggestion.

Then, a few days later, she fell out of her wheelchair while sitting at the nursing station. She would often try to stand up but couldn't do it on her own. I think it was after that fall that her mind started going. Her conversations became unrealistic. When not in the wheelchair, they had her sit at a table in the main room.

Usually, she had a cup of coffee in her hand when I came to visit. I had bought her a container of her favorite half and half, but, "Someone else must be using it," she told me rather calmly. "It doesn't last very long." I felt that she was giving up and giving in—nothing like the feisty woman I knew.

Of the other patients surrounding her, most sat very quietly with their heads down on the table, looking groggy. The exception was one woman who constantly groaned and struggled to get out of her chair. No restraints were ever used to my knowledge as they were illegal. But there was some kind of alarm on her chair whenever she tried to get up. In short, it was a very depressive atmosphere. Mom had no one to talk to.

At the suggestion of my friend Sheila, I contacted the Long-Term Care Ombudsmen Program, part of the Office of the Aging in New York State. They sent an advocate to speak to Mom.

"I'm here for you," Constance told her. "If you need any help, you can talk to me and I will discuss it with the nursing home staff. Or you can tell your daughter and she can call me." Although Mom was very appreciative, she didn't register any complaints.

Then she had another fall. I'm not exactly sure how, but she fell on her face, was very scratched up, and had injured her arm. The nursing home let me know that she had fallen and was in the hospital, but I didn't get to the hospital to see her, and I still have some occasional pangs of guilt: in my possession was a ticket for *The Nutcracker Suite,* the famous ballet at Lincoln Center. I was on my way there when I got the call. That ballet was going to be my escape from the stress and depression I was experiencing. I found myself very conflicted. I wanted desperately to see the performance, but questioned my decision, so I called my sister in Arizona.

"What do you think I should do?" I asked her. She knew how stressed I was, so she supported my desire.

"I think you should go. You need it. Everything has been falling on your shoulders. You can go to the hospital afterwards." Her answer gave me the permission I felt I needed to go to the show. Later on, when I rushed to see her, she had already been returned to the nursing home. I knew that I had let her down. I could see it in her eyes. The next time I went to see her, she was asleep in her wheelchair, sitting in her room. As I entered, a creak in the floor woke her up.

"Hi, Mom," I said.

"Who is this woman? Get her out of my room!" she shouted when she saw me. I ran crying from the room. In my mind, she had turned her mind off in order to avoid her current reality. Still, it stung when she said that about me, her devoted daughter. It still brings tears to my eyes that she had to suffer that way. An independent, still-vibrant woman such as she had been, had lost complete control of her environment.

An appointment was made to see the surgeon, post operation for her arm. They arranged for an ambulance to take her to the doctor on West 57th Street, and I rode with her.

"You are doing fine, recovery is good," the doctor reported. We sat in the waiting room for a long time, waiting for the ride back.

"Here's the sandwich they gave you, Mom. You must be hungry," I said, handing it to her. It was peanut butter and jelly, which she had never eaten before. She just gummed it, making no attempt to actually chew or eat it, seeming totally out of it.

"Maybe this is a good way for me to die. I'll just stop eating." *Is that what she's thinking?* I wondered.

Not long after that, the social worker called me. "Your mother's medical coverage will be ending soon. She will need full time care to go back to her apartment. Up until now, her health insurance has covered her care here, but now that she no longer gets physical therapy, she's not covered anymore."

"But why have they stopped her physical therapy?" I asked. "Can't they continue to provide the service?"

"They did an eval and determined that she would not benefit any longer from the therapy, so her insurance has closed her claim," she retorted. I tried to fight it, but meanwhile I was advised that she would have to leave the facility. I concurred that she would need twenty-four-hour care at home since she was unable to walk, but she had no coverage for that. If she remained at Amsterdam House, she would be covered by Medicaid. If she gave up her apartment at Manhattan Plaza, she would not be able to return. I alone felt the burden to make the difficult decision, although I'm sure I consulted with my children. My sister agreed with my thinking as well. So, the decision was made. Mom never asked when she would go home. I explained it to her and she accepted it. She accepted the reality, but I was still very stressed. It appeared to me that dementia was setting in. At times, her words were not logical. I felt helpless about the whole situation. I guess I myself wasn't accepting the reality.

Two weeks later, I received a call from the nurse at Amsterdam House after midnight.

"Your mother's blood pressure has been dropping. She's been taken to Roosevelt Hospital." Brian, my son, and I rushed over there. I had hailed a taxi and picked him up on the way.

She was agitated when we arrived, but not fully conscious. I tried to talk with her, but she couldn't answer, although I think she wanted to. We both just kept repeating, "We love you," over and over, hoping she was able to understand us.

"We are giving her something to relax her," the doctor told us. We stayed with her for a long time, but when she appeared to calm down, we decided to go home for a couple hours and made plans to come back early in the morning. But the next morning, the hospital called to tell me that she had passed away. The irony was that she had lived alone and sadly, was alone until the end.

Mom had just turned one hundred and five. I had anticipated her death so many times over the years that I think I had steeled my emotions in preparation for losing her. So I didn't cry then. Not until later on.

Mom's funeral was held at the Riverside Memorial Chapel, officiated by the rabbi from the Actor's Temple. Over the years, Mom had become an atheist, but she was also a woman proud of her history and Jewish heritage.

"Would you like a rabbi to speak at your funeral?" I had asked her years earlier.

"Yes, I would like that," she answered me.

Many other family members and I also spoke, offering up a celebration of Mom's life. The room was filled to the brim with family, friends, and neighbors.

"What's your secret?" people would often ask her. From her humble beginnings with a limited education, Mom had been able to make her way through an ever-evolving world.

"Just do the same thing today as you did yesterday. That's what I do," she'd answer.

But it wasn't as simple as that to me. To me, it was her positive attitude, persistence, curiosity, desire to learn, and her acceptance of change that made her so resilient. These were the attributes which provided her with the ability to enjoy life and thrive throughout her many years.

Acknowledgements

IT'S TAKEN A WHILE TO get this completed and I would like to recognize those who helped me.

Thanks to the women in my writing group for listening and offering suggested changes: Judy Rosner, Betsy Freedman, Debra Banerjee, Suzanne Chait, and Micheline Haas. Judy also came up with what I think is the perfect book title. Ronnie Miller provided writing advice.

Jaime Cox from Citrine Publishing Company has been an excellent editor. Thanks to Penelope Love of Citrine Publishing for the creation of this book. And of course, thank you to my family and friends for their consistent support.

And I dedicate this book to my sister, Penny, who I love and miss.

Publisher's Note

Thank you for the opportunity to serve you. If you would like to help share this message, here are some popular ways:

- **REVIEWS:** Write an online book review and tag #105yearsyoung and #corahoberman

- **GIVING:** Gift the book to your friends, family and colleagues

- **BOOK CLUBS:** Request a Reading Group Guide and an author visit: Info@CitrinePublishing.com

- **SPEAKING:** Invite Cora Hoberman to speak with your group: Info@CitrinePublishing.com

- **BULK ORDERS:** Call +1-828-585-7030 or email: Sales@CitrinePublishing.com

We appreciate your book reviews, letters, and shares.

www.ingramcontent.com/pod-product-compliance
Lightning Source LLC
Chambersburg PA
CBHW060527080526
44586CB00012B/653